Better Homes and Gardens®

YOUR WINDOWS & DOORS

BETTER HOMES AND GARDENS® BOOKS

Editor: Gerald M. Knox
Art Director: Ernest Shelton
Managing Editor: David A. Kirchner

Associate Art Directors: Linda Ford Vermie,
Neoma Alt West, Randall Yontz
Copy and Production Editors: Marsha Jahns,
Nancy Nowiszewski, Mary Helen Schiltz, David A. Walsh
Assistant Art Directors: Harijs Priekulis, Tom Wegner
Senior Graphic Designers: Alisann Dixon, Lynda Haupert,
Lyne Neymeyer
Graphic Designers: Mike Burns, Mike Eagleton, Deb Miner,
Stan Sams, D. Greg Thompson, Darla Whipple, Paul Zimmerman

Editor in Chief: Neil Kuehnl
Group Editorial Services Director: Duane L. Gregg

General Manager: Fred Stines
Director of Publishing: Robert B. Nelson
Vice President, Retail Marketing: Jamie Martin
Vice President, Direct Marketing: Arthur Heydendael

All About Your House: Your Windows and Doors

Project Editor: James A. Hufnagel
Associate Editor: Willa Rosenblatt Speiser
Assistant Editor: Leonore A. Levy
Copy and Production Editor: Mary Helen Schiltz
Building and Remodeling Editor: Joan McCloskey
Furnishings and Design Editor: Shirley Van Zante
Garden Editor: Douglas A. Jimerson
Money Management and Features Editor: Margaret Daly

Associate Art Director: Linda Ford Vermie
Graphic Designer: Stan Sams

Contributing Editor: Jean LemMon
Contributing Senior Writer: Paul Kitzke
Contributors: Denise L. Caringer, Lawrence D. Clayton,
Jim Harrold, Jill Mead, Stephen Mead,
Peter Stephano

Special thanks to William N. Hopkins, Bill Hopkins, Jr.,
Babs Klein, and Don Wipperman for their valuable
contributions to this book.

INTRODUCTION

Your home's windows and doors work something like Alice's looking glass: They can bring in light, air, views, and people—or they can shut them all out. Versatile space dividers, windows and doors can either connect or separate your family's private domain from the world outside.

Your Windows and Doors takes a close look at these functional designs. First, it raises a series of questions about what your windows and doors do now, and what you'd like them to do. Next, it presents a portfolio of styles that can help you match windows and doors to your home, your needs, and your budget.

How you decorate windows and doors reflects both your taste and their function. Three chapters delve into the basics of selecting, planning, and executing successful window and door treatments.

If your house is an older one, its windows and doors may be rattling or sticking in their frames, wasting energy, or simply not looking their best. Replacing them with easy-to-operate, snug, attractive new units is easier than you might think. We take you step-by-step through the process, and also show how new windows, skylights, bump-outs, and bays can brighten your outlook. Energy and security also are important topics around most of today's households, so each gets a chapter of its own.

Finally, we've put together hard-working pages of maintenance, repair, and cleaning information to help you keep your windows squeaky clean and your door hinges squeak-free.

We hope *Your Windows and Doors,* like other volumes in the **ALL ABOUT YOUR HOUSE** Library, will open up new ways to make your home more attractive, comfortable, functional, and uniquely your own.

YOUR WINDOWS AND DOORS

CONTENTS

CHAPTER 6

UPGRADING WINDOWS AND DOORS 82

CHAPTER 7

SAVE ENERGY 98

CHAPTER 8

SECURING YOUR HOME 114

CHAPTER 9

LET IN MORE LIGHT 124

CHAPTER 10

REPAIRING AND MAINTAINING WINDOWS AND DOORS 140

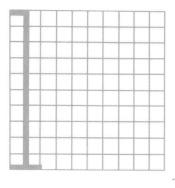

SIZING UP YOUR HOME'S WINDOWS AND DOORS

When you stand in front of your house—or any other—the windows and main entry door should be among the first things you notice. Windows and doors whose size, shape, and style are consistent with each other and with the exterior appearance of the house make a good first impression. Even more important is what they do for the rooms inside. The trade-offs you make between views and privacy, for example, or light and energy conservation, can be as important as architectural considerations. This chapter raises a variety of questions about your windows and doors—how they work, what they look like, and the jobs you'd like them to do better. Once you've decided which questions are most relevant to your house, turn to the chapters that follow for the answers.

FIRST, ASSESS THE GLASS AREAS AT YOUR HOUSE

One look at the living room *at right* is clear evidence that glass can be an incomparable building material. Here, the large-paned windows soar to the ceiling of a double-height room. Because the house is built on a heavily wooded site, privacy is not a factor. What does matter is the view—the grandeur of the trees is echoed by vertical-grained Douglas fir posts that frame the windows and French doors. The result: a space almost as spectacular as nature.

Glass can be a great mood-setter in just about any room. When the sun is shining, glass sparkles and lets in light and warmth. It brings the outdoors in—if you want it to. It creates a style almost by itself. For example, a wall of sliding glass doors and stationary glazed panels is an instantly recognizable contemporary feature; an equal expanse of double-hung multipane windows or mullioned casements creates a totally different look. For more about this, see Chapter 2—"A Portfolio of Window and Door Designs."

For all its virtues, however, glass is not perfect. Where privacy is important, expanses of glass need to be screened and supplemented by window treatments of some kind. Even double- or triple-glazed glass is a relatively poor insulating material in comparison to an insulated frame wall. For help in treating problem windows, see Chapters 3 and 5; to learn about conserving energy without giving up the advantages of large windows, see Chapter 7. If you'd like to make more of the glass at your house and need ideas, see Chapter 6—"Upgrading Windows and Doors"—and Chapter 9—"Let In More Light."

DO YOU RELY ON NATURAL LIGHT FOR MOOD?

Enter a room sparkling with bright sunlight and you feel charged and exhilarated. Picture the same space bathed in a soft, filtered glow, and the mood becomes peaceful and calming. Reduce incoming light still further and the room takes on a mysterious cast. Weather and the shifting angles of the sun present an ever-changing play of light through your windows. Sit back and watch the whole performance through bare windows, or select window treatments that let you be the director.

Light—and the shadows created by it—are as much decorative elements in a room as your wall covering or furnishings. As the sun shifts, it subtly changes the shapes and patterns in a room. To make the most of this natural kaleidoscope, plan a furniture arrangement that allows open floor and/or wall space for shadow play.

In the living room *at right*, furniture is pulled in from the windows to allow light to flow unobstructed. The bare wood floor shows off shadows cast by the multipaned windows.

Let the sun shine in

To decorate with light, you'll want to be able to let as much in as possible. This usually means leaving windows bare, or choosing window coverings that can be drawn completely aside or adjusted to let light stream in unfiltered. On pages 68 and 69, you'll see how one couple struck a balance between the light-filled den they wanted and the privacy they sometimes needed. If your existing doors and windows don't admit as much light as you'd like, turn to Chapter 9—"Let In More Light"—for information about adding skylights, cantilevered windows, and other sun-catchers.

Color your world

The color of sunlight never changes, but the shades you decorate with make it *appear* different. Reds, oranges, and yellows accentuate the sun-drenched feeling. Blues, greens, and violets cool it down.

For very sunny rooms, earth tones and neutrals, like those in the room *at right*, may be your best bet. Strong sunlight fades most colors, but you'll notice it less with earth tones.

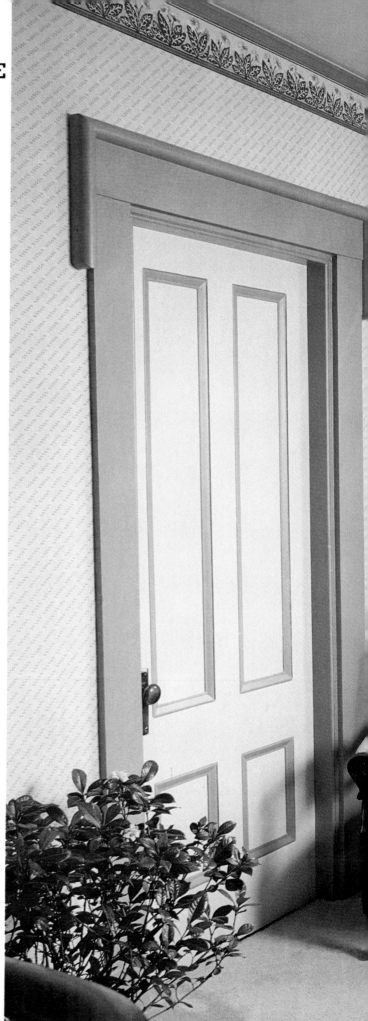

SIZING UP YOUR HOME'S WINDOWS AND DOORS

DO YOU WANT TO EMPHASIZE DOORS AND WINDOWS?

Windows can be beautiful. Not just the view you see through them, or the treatment you've given them, but the windows themselves. The unique architectural character of windows—and doors, too—is reason enough to give them top billing in your decorating scheme. You may want to play them up because of their dramatic placement. Or perhaps, as with leaded windows, the glass itself is unusual. If your windows and doors are worthy of notice, cast them as design elements in their own right.

To spotlight window or door units, eliminate competition. Steer clear of distracting treatments that mask their features. Instead, bring out natural characteristics with decorative accents. Use a contrasting paint color to detail molding or accentuate the shape of the woodwork, as shown *at right*.

Choose a wall covering or paint color that complements and supports your window and door treatments. Allow for some breathing room—wall accessories hung too close to windows and doors will draw attention away from them.

Keep the area in front of the windows free of furniture. Very often it's the proportion of the units that gives them their grace and beauty. Interrupting the flow of a window's lines diminishes the impact.

If you choose to draw attention to your windows and doors, they should be in excellent condition and sparkling clean. Chapter 10—"Repairing and Maintaining Windows and Doors"—shows how to keep them at their best.

Disappearing acts

What if your windows and doors are far from spectacular? One option is to downplay them: Treat walls, windows, and doors with a similar color or pattern so the units seem to disappear into the walls. Or emphasize the treatment instead of the unit itself. (More about this in Chapter 3—"Treat Your Windows"—and Chapter 5—"Planning Window Treatments.")

If units with a bit more architectural flair would enhance your decorating scheme, turn to add-on details for help. On pages 26-27 and 32-33, you'll find a selection of ways to customize an ordinary window or door.

DO YOU REALLY WANT A WINDOW TREATMENT?

Sometimes the most effective window treatment is none at all. Perhaps you have a view of trees and hilltops, or a less-than-spectacular view framed by finely proportioned and interestingly detailed windows. In cases like these, sparkling panes may be all the window dressing you need most of the time. For occasional privacy or light control, an unobtrusive roll-up shade or blind, concealed behind a cornice, may do the job. If you think this "undecorating" possibility might appeal to you, read on.

Once you've begun to think of window treatments in an "if" rather than "what kind of" way, review the case *for* window treatments—and the case against them. We'll start with some reasons you might want to do without dressy window treatments, or any at all.

The case against window coverings

There are situations where window treatments may just be in the way. See how many of these apply to your home and taste.

• Your window architecture and woodwork are too attractive or unusual to cover with fabric or any other treatment.

• You have a lush crop of foliage outside the window (as in the photograph *at left*). Foliage, besides being nice to look at, forms a natural privacy screen, and the shapes of leaves—or winter branches—form patterns in your glass and shadows on your walls as attractive as most man-made designs. The privacy may be seasonal if the trees and shrubs are deciduous, but the branches may be dense enough to provide some screening even in winter.

• You have a view that rivals a postcard. It's too good to hide. In this case, you may even want to expand your vista with bigger windows, as explained in Chapter 6—"Upgrading Windows and Doors."

• You like as much natural light as possible, and all but the simplest window treatment would defeat your purpose.

• Your room looks larger without window coverings and this illusion of space is important to you.

The case for window treatments

It may be that stripped-down windows are not for you. Here are some reasons why you may decide to do more for your windows than just keep them clean.

• You like privacy or have unusually "public" windows. Treatments can cover a window for privacy yet give you some control over the view outside and the light that comes in.

• You're concerned about energy loss. Glass conducts both heat and cold, and if your windows are placed where their lack of insulation plays havoc with your heating and cooling bills, plan a covering that will help you control these costs. To learn more about saving energy, see Chapter 7.

• You want to control the amount of light that comes in. Glare can be a problem even on overcast days. If that's the case with some of your windows, plan treatments that let you control light—both the amount and quality.

• Your windows are small or awkwardly placed. A well-planned window treatment can expand, contract, organize, or emphasize.

• Your room and its windows are lacking in character and you want to add some. Window treatments provide color, texture, pattern—even a sense of architecture.

• You want to coordinate your furniture coverings with other elements in the room. A fabric treatment is a logical way to tie a room together.

• Your room is cavernous and you want to make it cozier. A space-taking window treatment, especially combined with a darker wall covering, is a viable solution.

WHAT KIND
OF WINDOW TREATMENT
DO YOU WANT?

If the case *for* window treatments on the preceding page convinced you, you still have a lot of choices to make. A window treatment can be anything from a roller shade that blocks out the too-early morning sun to a triple-tiered valance and drapery confection. Shutters, screens, and combinations of assorted individual treatments are all part of the category. What kind of window treatment you need is determined not just by the functions you want it to serve, but also by the look you want to achieve and the mood you want to create. On these two pages, we'll start you thinking about ways to pull all these considerations together to plan a treatment that's right for your home.

In this living room, the window treatment takes center stage. A pair of Mexican screens, framed with tin and patterned with mirrors and translucent glass, transforms this '30s bungalow into an atmospheric hideaway.

Everything here was carefully chosen to create a special ambience, yet the owners were faced with a jarring commercial district virtually in their own front yard. The screens solved that problem by partially obscuring the view, which keeps the activity outside from intruding on the private world inside. The table, with its plant and lamp, fills the gap between the screens, yet lets unfiltered light in through the windows.

Though this treatment is highly individual, the decorating problems it solves are familiar ones—how to ensure privacy without blocking light and how to integrate windows into an overall design scheme. A more traditional approach might use richly patterned draw draperies to reinforce the warm, deep tones of the rug and furniture, and sheer underdraperies to filter light and soften the view.

Job description
The first step in deciding what window treatments are best for you is to decide what you want them to do. If light control and privacy are your main concerns, then a roller shade or mini-slat blind is the most basic answer—supplemented, perhaps, by a decorative fabric treatment. If you're worried about energy loss, then woven woods may be what you're looking for. If you are primarily interested in perking up a room's looks or carrying out an existing decorating theme, your choices are practically limitless.

Treatments that work only for a specific window may not suit your life-style, or traditional fabric treatments may not be to your taste. If this is the case, take one more look at the photo *at left* and you'll see that the screens are, in fact, a free-standing, portable window treatment. Portables can be dealt with as furniture, packed and delivered to your next address, or moved just as easily from room to room for a change of interior scene.

Chapter 3—"Treat Your Windows"—surveys a wide range of window treatments to help you familiarize yourself with your options.

Next, consider the window

Once you've thought about treatments and the jobs you want them to do, think about the kind of window you'll be decorating. A mini-slat blind may be great for light control, but if the window in question is an in-swinging casement, installation will be tricky— although with careful planning it can be done. Chapter 2— "A Portfolio of Window and Door Designs"—provides an overview that will start you on your way to understanding the decorating needs of your own windows and doors.

Once you put together the kinds of windows you have in your house and the kinds of jobs you want your window treatments to perform, then taste, budget, and life-style are the major considerations. In the first 10 pages of Chapter 5— "Planning Window Treatments"—you'll see how five families selected window treatments that met their particular window-decorating needs. The rest of Chapter 5 presents a sketchbook of alternative window treatments for different kinds of windows. At least one of them may be for you.

HOW IMPORTANT IS YOUR ENTRY?

What does your entry say about you and your family? Like a handshake, it can be a strong initial indicator of how friendly and hospitable you are. Besides making a good first impression and serving as a place to leave snowy boots and wet shoes, your entry can do more. Entries come in myriad shapes and sizes, from grand foyers to standing-room-only vestibules. Help yours put all its square footage to use, whether as an art gallery, a gracious receiving area for guests, or simply a small but well-decorated place where the welcome mat is on permanent display.

The entry *at left* is spectacular—large, sunlit, framed with massive oak timbers. It's enough to make anyone want to go out and put in a fanlight, paint the walls white, and open up the stairwell. That may, in fact, be a good idea for you. But there are many other possibilities, some much more modest in scope.

Before you start to plan any changes in your entry or think about adding a new one, consider it from several perspectives—space, architectural elements, function, and design.

Space
How large is the area just inside your door? How large should it be on the basis of the functions it serves? Is it a small vestibule with a coat closet opening off it? Is it the spacious center hallway of your house? Or is it totally nonexistent?

If the space does not meet your requirements, the next place to look is the adjoining room. Can you borrow a sliver of living room or dining room to create a more spacious entry?

If your front door opens directly into a living area with no distinct entry, you might want to split off a space, define it with walls or dividers, and create a new space.

Architectural elements
All entries have a few features in common, notably a door and perhaps a window. Choosing these elements well is the first step toward creating an entry that does more than just let people into the house. Consider replacing a standard door with one that offers more design. Pages 92-95 explain how to do the work.

If the entry area is windowless, a new window would add something special. Flank a door with sidelights, or add a fanlight, and maybe a transom, over the door. Decorative window units do more than make your entry more attractive—they provide light and, if you choose, ventilation. Adding glass to an entry is a great way to make it look bigger than it is.

For more about door and window styles and arrangements, see Chapter 2—"A Portfolio of Window and Door Designs."

Function
How an entry is used or is intended to be used has a lot to do with whether it's large enough—or seems large enough. If you want a table for mail and gloves, a mirror for last-minute primping, and a hall tree for extra outerwear, you'd better have an entry with plenty of floor space.

Your entry can also amplify the design and decorating theme in the rest of your house. If it's large enough, it can become an adjunct to entertainment areas or a storage place for attractive photographs, books, or other objects of visual interest.

Decorating
The door is usually the largest and most important component of the entry; choose a design treatment that lives up to it. Hardware, fabric treatments, and the door itself are all highly noticeable—and variable—factors. See Chapter 4—"Decorate Your Doors"—for more about dressing your entry door for any occasion.

SIZING UP YOUR HOME'S WINDOWS AND DOORS

HOW SECURE ARE YOUR WINDOWS AND DOORS?

Is your home an easy target for a break-in artist? Or would it at least put up a good struggle to keep one out? Windows and doors are any home's most vulnerable points of entry. In many cases, they're so accessible that breaking and entering doesn't even require breaking. The key to security is common sense mixed with caution. Start with a survey of your doors and windows to see how securely they stand between your home and unwelcome visitors.

If someone is really determined to break into your house, chances are it can be done. But there are several practical steps you can take to keep out intruders. These steps fall into three categories: first, discourage even the thought of a break-in; second, deter the entering process; and finally, scare the intruder away with an alarm system. To get an idea of where to start, take a security inventory of your home, as explained on pages 114 and 115.

For example, an inventory of the house *at right* turned up several lapses in security. Shrubbery and shadows make good hiding places near doors and windows, so foundation plantings were cut back. The windows themselves are large and easy to enter through, so they were secured with key-operated locks. Since the large tree provides easy access to second-story windows via the porch, those windows were also fitted with locks. Pages 116-118 tell more about protecting windows.

Next, take a critical look at your doors. At this house, glass flanking the entry could be broken for access to the interior latch. A double-cylinder lock was the answer. To learn more about protecting doors, see pages 119-121; to learn about choosing and installing new, sturdier doors, turn to pages 88-97.

If a determined intruder maneuvers past these preventive devices, a wailing, ringing, ear-splitting alarm will likely chase him away. Installing an alarm system is a good investment in personal safety and property protection, but there are also some drawbacks. Pages 122 and 123 tell about the pros and cons of home alarm systems and give a rundown of the various types.

HOW ENERGY EFFICIENT ARE YOUR WINDOWS AND DOORS?

Is your house a bit *too* much like a castle—invaded by icy drafts? And does it take a king's ransom to pay your utility bills? If so, your windows and doors probably share a good part of the blame. Glass itself is a poor insulator, offering little resistance to heat transfer. Set it into ill-fitting windows and doors that leak air, and energy loss is even greater. You can attack energy waste on two fronts. Improve windows and doors themselves, and then add energy-conserving treatments.

Just standing in front of one of your windows or doors will give you a general idea of how energy efficient it is. An energy audit performed by your utility company will give you a more precise assessment.

If your windows and doors rate poorly, several factors are involved. The direction a window or door faces definitely influences the amount of heat or cold it is exposed to. Unless you're building a new home, or extensively remodeling, you'll have to live with units where they are, but page 98 will tell you how to take placement into account to save energy.

No matter where a window is located, its construction influences its energy efficiency. Double-glazed windows, or triple-glazed units like the ones used in the solar home *at left*, provide good barriers against winter cold and summer heat. It often makes sense to replace less-efficient single-glazed windows with double glazing and/or storm windows. Chapter 6 tells how to save energy by upgrading windows and doors.

Saving with treatments

Are you breezing along with nothing but flimsy fabric at your windows? If so, you're missing the added insulation an energy-efficient treatment can provide. Even an economical roller shade helps reduce heat loss. Page 100 will show you an especially efficient way to install one. Look to interior and exterior shading systems, and reflective and insulated draperies. Chapter 7—"Save Energy"—gives you decorating ideas and buymanship facts on a cross section of these energy-saving window products.

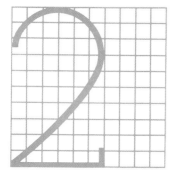

A PORTFOLIO OF WINDOW AND DOOR DESIGNS

Windows and exterior doors are the eyes of a house. They let in light and air, give personality to the whole, and play a large part in determining what your home looks like from the outside. By providing a view of the outdoors, windows and doors also influence the interior ambience. On the following pages, you'll learn about the many varieties of windows and doors, and the styles and uses with which they're most compatible.

Windows have long been among the most important components of any home. Both inside and out, they help define your home's appearance and shape its views. Because they often make up the major portion of a home's outside walls, they are a priority in any face-lifting project. In a new home, proper choice of windows may well be the key to a pleasant environment, energy efficiency, and lasting character.

Unlike yesterday's wood-framed windows, which were often made by hand, today's windows are manufactured to exacting specifications and come in a variety of materials.

Naming the parts

The basic components of all windows have the same names, but since some windows are mechanically simpler than others, not all have a full range of parts. Some windows, such as the "fixed lights" at the sides of doors or high on walls, are meant to remain closed, but most others have movable sashes and mechanical parts.

Identified on the opposite page are the various components of a standard double-hung window, the most complicated type and therefore the one with the most components. An explanation of each of its many parts and how each functions follows:
• The *sash* is the framework into which the *panes* (lights) are set. Double-hung windows have two sashes.
• Strips called *muntins* separate the panes. In older windows muntins are structural features; on newer windows they may simply be decorative removable grilles or absent entirely (see page 26 for more about muntins).

• *Jambs* form the sides and top of the window opening. Concealed behind the *side jambs* on older windows are heavy sash weights connected to the sashes with rope-and-pulley systems. The weights provide a counterbalance that makes the sashes easier to open. Rather than sash weights, newer windows use a revolving drum in the *head jamb* or tubed tension springs in the side jambs.
• A series of *stops* attached to the jambs provides channels in which the sashes can slide. *Blind stops* are permanently attached to the outside edges of the jambs, but both a *parting stop* and an *inside stop* can be pried loose to remove the sashes.
• A *sash lock* squeezes the sashes together, keeping the window securely closed and minimizing drafts where the sashes meet.
• *Interior trim,* or *casing,* at the sides and top and an *apron* across the bottom cover any gaps between jambs and walls.
• The *lower sash* comes to rest behind a flat *stool* or *interior sill;* its outside counterpart, the *exterior sill,* is sloped so water will run off.

Double-hung windows come as assembled units, except for the casing, apron, and stool, which are usually cut and fitted after the window is installed in the rough opening. To learn about installing double-hung windows, see pages 84 and 85; to learn about repairing them, see pages 147 and 148.

ANATOMY OF A DOUBLE-HUNG WINDOW

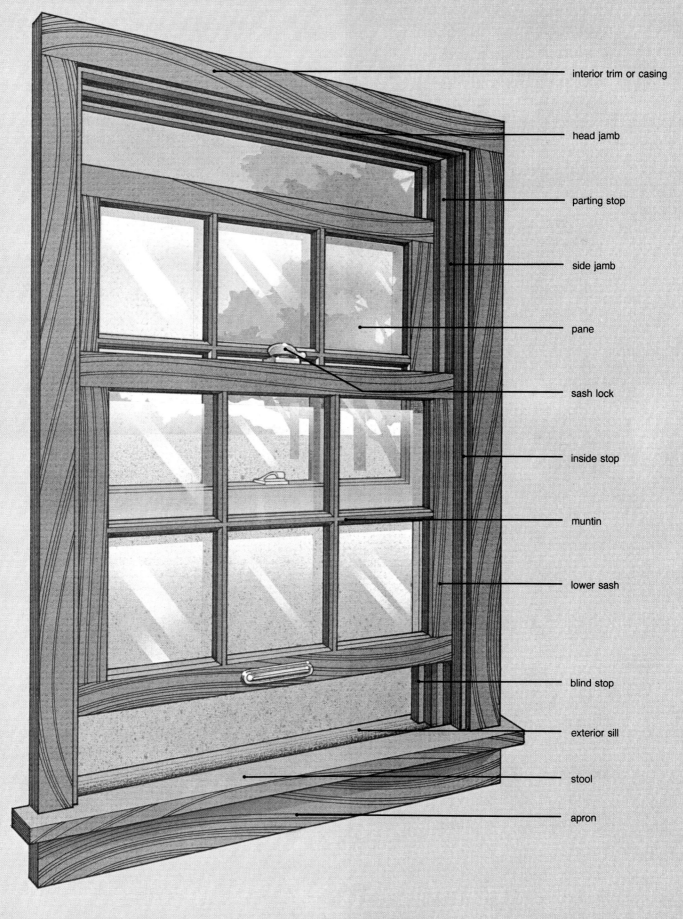

- interior trim or casing
- head jamb
- parting stop
- side jamb
- pane
- sash lock
- inside stop
- muntin
- lower sash
- blind stop
- exterior sill
- stool
- apron

WINDOW STYLES

Windows come in lots of shapes and sizes, and each will do the basic jobs you expect windows to do—let in light and, in most cases, air. But beyond that, you'll want to choose a window that looks right with your home's architectural style, whether that's clapboard colonial, redwood contemporary, or comfortable eclectic. And looks aside, each type of window has its advantages and disadvantages. Knowing what they are will help you choose the right windows for any remodeling or building project.

Early builders chose windows according to the number of panes in each sash—six over six, for example, or nine over 12. Today your choices are much broader. Casements, awnings, sliders, hoppers, jalousies, fixed glass, and combinations of all these styles pose a myriad of alternatives to the classic double-hung window. Here are the factors you'll want to consider.

The amount of air a window brings in may be very important to you. Casement windows, for example, because they swing out, can be operated to catch breezes that might otherwise pass on by.

Of course, the amount of light any type of window will admit depends largely on its size. But shape and where you locate a window do make a difference. For example, a horizontal window placed high on a wall may provide more light than the same window turned vertically.

Ease of cleaning is also worth thinking about, especially if yours is a two-story house or if some of the windows are just hard to reach. A many-paned window is more difficult to clean than one large sheet of glass. A reversible or removable sash that can be washed conveniently from the inside makes it a lot easier—and safer—to keep upper-story windows sparkling.

Sashes on the move
Windows can be categorized by the ways in which their sashes operate. Here's a rundown of the most common variations.

• *Double-hung windows* have two sashes that bypass each other vertically in channels of the frame. (See pages 22 and 23 for more about the parts of these windows.) Normally, double-hung windows open from both the top and bottom. Sash weights, a tension spring, or a revolving drum system holds them open. Glazing is either unobstructed or divided by muntins. The versatile design of double-hung windows makes them appropriate for traditional housing styles as well as for some split-level and ranch-style homes. Their ease of operation is a plus, but, fully open, the sashes block half the opening, which limits ventilation.

• *Casements* consist of a single sash or a pair of sashes hinged vertically along the outer jamb(s). They open by means of a crank or lever and provide maximum ventilation. Multipane casements add a charming old-fashioned look to certain period homes; yet the clean, simple look of one-pane casements is ideal for contemporary homes. Casements also are easy to clean. Newer versions usually have integral storms and screens, but older ones require cumbersome interior storms and screens.

• *Sliding windows* have two sashes that move horizontally in a common frame. Since they can be conveniently used high on a wall, they're a good way to provide plenty of light and limited ventilation without sacrificing privacy and wall space.

• *Awning windows* have a single sash hinged to open up and out from the sill by means of a geared crank or slide bar. An extending arm hinge holds them in position. Used in combination with fixed glass, awnings are well suited to the lines of ranch-style homes. One unique feature is that you can leave them open in all but a driving rain. They're easy to clean, provide good ventilation, and most have integral storms and screens. Awnings do catch dirt and debris from above, however.

• *Hopper windows,* hinged at the bottom, operate like upside-down awning windows. Because of their poor ventilating qualities and vulnerability to rain and snow, their use is limited to special applications, such as below-grade basements.

• *Jalousies* consist of a series of heavy glass panels that pivot outward simultaneously by means of a geared handle. They allow maximum ventilation but are hard to clean and insulate. They're often used for porches.

• *Fixed-glass windows* do not open; they consist of a large, single expanse of glazing set into a frame. Contemporary homes often use fixed glass for passive solar heating. High glazing replacement cost, difficulty of exterior cleaning, and insulating problems are its major disadvantages.

Combinations
Bows, bays, and clerestories are not window types but assemblies of any of the preceding sashes. Combinations of casements and fixed glass or double-hung and fixed units are the most common.

• A *bow window* is a series of sashes bumped out from the house in a segmented arch. It's usually covered by the eave or its own roof.

• A *bay window* normally has a fixed-glass center section flanked by two operative sashes that return to the house wall at 45- or 30-degree angles.

• A *clerestory* (pronounced "clear story") is typically made up of a series of fixed-glass or sliding windows. It directs light from a point—usually high on a wall—to a room or area that would otherwise be without natural light.

casement

bow

bay

clerestory

double-hung

sliding

awning

jalousie

hopper

fixed

CUSTOMIZING WINDOWS

With windows, details—or a lack of them—make all the difference. Traditional styles such as Georgian or New England saltbox rely upon muntins, shutters, semicircular fanlights, and assorted moldings for character and visual interest. Consider these same elements to complement your windows. Here's an illustrated survey of the main possibilities.

Look through the millwork catalog at a well-stocked lumberyard and you'll find a wide array of window dressings. One or a combination of these components can give your windows a custom look.

Muntins

Muntins, those small framing members that divide the panes of glass in a sash, are an effective first step in defining certain architectural styles. Years ago, when window glass was weaker, muntins served to bind individual panes together. Muntins are no longer needed for strength, but yesterday's charm is almost instantly attainable by using snap-in muntin grilles.

Ready-made versions, available in rectangular- and diamond-pane configurations, give the same overall effect as the originals—with the added benefit that you can easily remove the grilles to clean the window. If you have standard-size newer windows, check with a local dealer for snap-in units. If your windows are older or an unusual size, you may have to custom-make muntin grilles.

Shutters

Shutters are another detail that, along with muntins, emphasize and complete a traditional architectural look. Long before storm windows and heavy window glass were available, shutters protected thin window panes and kept homes draft-free.

Originally, shutters were closed to create a blanket of insulating air space between the window and the outside. Heat-robbing cold air was kept out in winter, and in summer, uncomfortable warm air was blocked. To perform either of these functions, the shutters had to completely cover the

MUNTINS

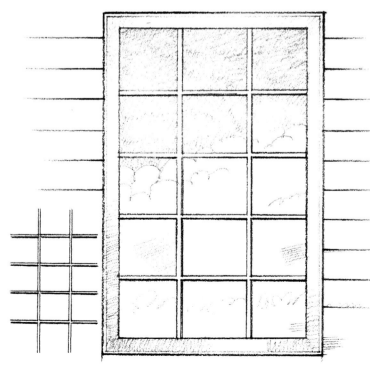

SHUTTERS

FANLIGHT

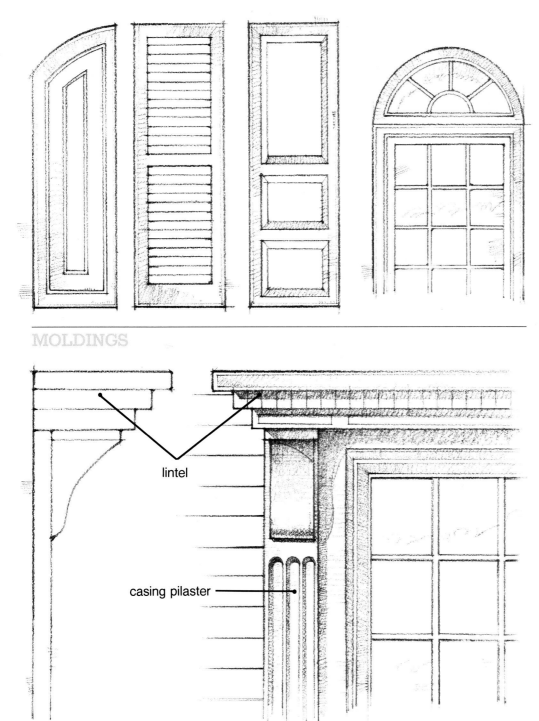

MOLDINGS

lintel

casing pilaster

window. Therefore, to be authentic-looking, your shutters, too, should be of a size that will do just that.

Traditional wooden shutters are still around, but shutters made of low-maintenance, weather-resistant polystyrene also are available. You'll find these updated shutters molded in wood-grain textures in a variety of basic colors.

If you don't care about shutters that actually open and close, it's easy to attach them with screws. But operable shutters require good-quality hinges that allow them to swing into position smoothly and be conveniently removed for cleaning.

Fanlights

Arched *fanlights,* widely used in earlier eras, are still made by a number of window manufacturers. Available as separate units that can be installed above existing windows, fanlights add a special touch, as do complete round-topped new windows. Glazing options include clear, tinted, and stained glass. Fanlights also come in several patterns, available with either solid spoke dividers or removable muntin grids. To complete the exterior effect, add curved-head shutters to accent the graceful new windows.

Moldings

Look closely at the moldings on old houses, and you'll discover that most of those elaborate curves and relief work were built up by piecing together separate, simpler elements to make one spectacular whole. Consider duplicating Greek revival or Georgian details such as the carved *lintels* and columnlike *casing pilasters* shown *at left.*

GETTING TO KNOW DOORS

Your front door may very well be the first—if not the most—noticed design element in your home. A good front door reflects both your taste and your home's design and decorating themes. Of course, matching and complementary interior doors accent your decorating statement. Consider doors as carefully as you would carpeting or wallpaper, so your choice fits not just your door frame but your own style.

Doors are constructed in one of two ways—with separate panels, like the *panel door* illustrated *opposite,* or with a flat face, like the *flush doors* shown *below.* Very few doors consist of nothing but a single slab of wood; even if door-size planks were widely available, these would soon warp out of shape.

Essentially, all panel doors consist of stiles, rails, and panels.

• *Stiles* serve as the vertical framing members on each side of the door. The one on the lock side is the *lock stile;* the other is the *hinge stile.*

• *Rails* form the top and bottom horizontal framing members; a center rail, called the *lock rail,* is part of many but not all designs.

• *Panels* are the areas framed by the rails. They may match the rest of the door, or they may be glass or some other material.

Putting the pieces together

Different configurations of these door elements define a door's architectural character. Many doors, for example, have stiles and rails that form a Christian cross—a simple design that has been passed down from early days, when doors were often made to reflect their owners' religious beliefs. (See pages 30 and 31 for a look at some of the other possibilities for panel door designs.)

Door hardware, too, is effective in defining style. Heavy hinges support the door's weight, but also can be highly decorative. Similarly, a knob set with a keylock and dead bolt offers protection and an interesting metal highlight. (For more about door hardware, see pages 32 and 33, 96 and 97, and 119-121.)

Flush doors

Flush doors consist of a surface covering over either a *solid* or *hollow core.* Examine the drawings *below* and you'll notice that flush doors also have rails and stiles that are concealed by the facing material. To minimize warping, wood doors are faced with two or more layers of veneer.

But not all flush doors are made of wood alone. They can also be clad with vinyl-covered wood, aluminum, or steel, among other materials.

Under the facing, flush doors may include a core of dense hardwood or particleboard, or cellular material such as cardboard or foam.

Elements of a door frame

A door, whether exterior or interior, hangs in a frame that consists of several major elements.

• The *head jamb* is at the top, flanked by two *side jambs*—one on the lock side and one on the hinge side.

• The *saddle* or *threshold,* often eliminated on interior doors, lies underfoot.

• *Stops,* narrow strips of wood nailed to the head and side jambs, prevent the door from swinging past its hinges when it closes.

• The *strike plate,* a metal strip mortised into the side jamb on the lock side of the door, accepts the *latch.* (For more about latches, see pages 95-97.)

• *Casings* at the top and sides of interior and exterior doors complete the framework and add the finishing touch to the installation.

• *Weather stripping,* ideally incorporating interlocking metal strips, should be included all around the frame of a well-made exterior door.

To learn about choosing and installing doors, see pages 88-94.

ANATOMIES OF FLUSH DOORS

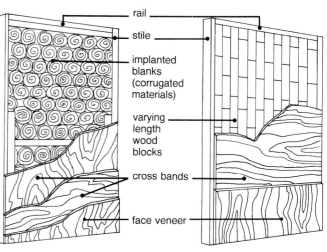

rail
stile
implanted blanks (corrugated materials)
varying length wood blocks
cross bands
face veneer

ANATOMY OF A PANEL DOOR

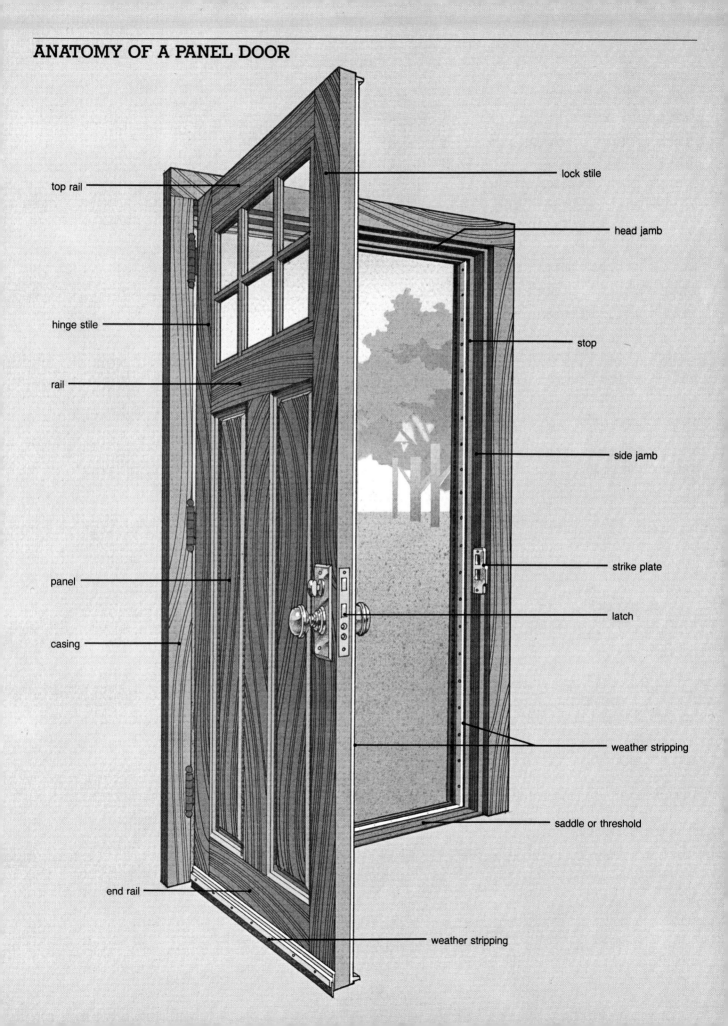

top rail

hinge stile

rail

panel

casing

end rail

lock stile

head jamb

stop

side jamb

strike plate

latch

weather stripping

saddle or threshold

weather stripping

French doors

5-panel door   15-panel door   half-acting door   louver door   combination door

DOOR STYLES

Doors not only serve as buffers between the world outside and the comfort of home, they also make your home more livable and appealing. Manufacturers produce doors in scores of shapes, sizes, colors, and materials. Browse through a supplier's catalog or explore your local lumberyard to spark your imagination. But first, look over the door styles shown and described on these pages and plan how to work them into your own building or remodeling project.

Choosing the right door for a front entry, service entrance, interior passage, or even a closet involves knowing where each kind of door works best and whether it will look right in a given location. On the preceding pages you learned about the two common types of doors. Here, let's take a look at some of the styles available in panel and flush doors. A panel door, for instance, may go well in a New England saltbox or a stuccoed Spanish ranch, depending on the number of panels and the character and extent of carved or applied details.

Panel door styles

Panel doors offer the widest variety of choices. Scan the examples shown here and you'll see doors with three, five, six, eight, and even 15 solid panels, in all sorts of shape and size combinations. What's more, the panels in a panel door needn't be made of solid material. In some entry doors, the upper panels are glass, and French doors have nothing but glass panes. Use these—inside or out— wherever you want to take advantage of views or light. French doors are often used in older homes to separate vestibules from hallways, or related rooms from each other.

• *Half-acting doors,* more commonly known as *Dutch doors,* have two independently operable sections, each capable of opening. When the two halves are fastened together, they operate as a unit. Normally, the top half is glazed, and the lower half has an X-shaped panel design. Dutch doors are useful where, in addition to the usual door function, ventilation is also important. Dutch doors can blend with many styles but are especially compatible with colonial and country looks.

• *Louver doors* consist of horizontal wooden or vinyl slats framed by stiles and rails. Used primarily as interior doors, they blend well with a variety of decors. They make special sense on closets and in other applications where ventilation is important and acoustic privacy is not.

• *Combination doors* are normally used outside primary exterior doors for insulation and weather protection. The top half contains removable glazing that can be replaced by a screen for ventilation. Some units have self-storing screen and glass. Wood and metal are common construction materials.

Flush door styles

Flush doors come in a more limited range of variations. Their simple lines lend themselves to many architectural styles, especially contemporary. To give a flush door a more traditional look, add moldings to its surface.

• *Patio,* or *sliding glass, doors* are a type of flush door. Usually, one panel is stationary and the other slides. Since these doors generally lead outside, their large expanses should be double-glazed. The frame may be wood, vinyl- or metal-clad wood, or aluminum.

FLUSH DOORS

sliding

flush

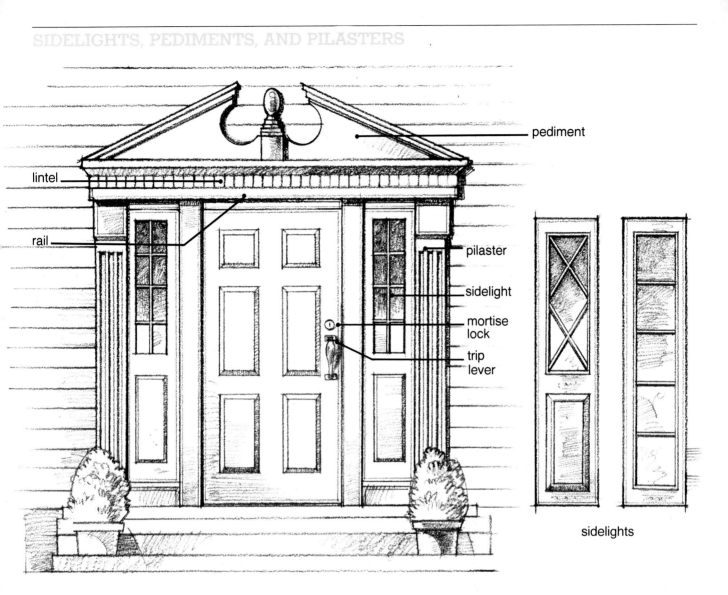

pediment

lintel

rail

pilaster

sidelight

mortise lock

trip lever

sidelights

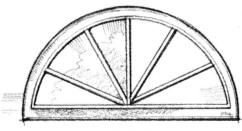

fanlight

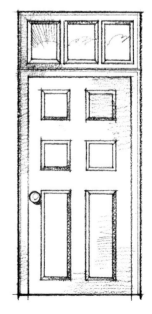

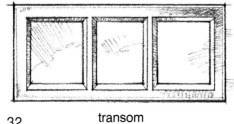

transom

CUSTOMIZING DOORS

A good-looking door is just the beginning of a welcoming entry. Even the most attractive door needs good details and accessories to make it stand out. Whether you use reproductions of original millwork or contemporary adaptations of classic designs, the range of trim available is extensive, and the use of economical modern materials such as formed vinyl and polystyrene puts accessories within reach of most budgets. Hardware details, too, add a flourish of style to your home's exterior and indoor doorways. You can buy millwork and other details from manufacturers and retail outlets, or you can assemble them from various stock elements.

Details and accessories designed to highlight a specific architectural style can help you individualize your entry. The examples on these two pages illustrate only a few of the attractive extras you can add to make your doors special.

Exterior details
Detail work to be used outside, whether it's made of vinyl, polystyrene, or wood, requires a good coat of exterior trim paint after installation. Except for glazed details, such as sidelights, which should be installed with the door, most details can be added after the rest of the door is in place.
• *Sidelights* (narrow windows flanking a door), *fanlights* (semicircular ribbed windows usually placed over a door), and *transoms* (horizontal windows placed directly above a door) used with an exterior door lend a gracious air to an entry and add natural light to a heavily used, but often dimly lit, area. All three must be allowed for when cutting in the rough door opening. The glazing may be plain or dressed up with muntins, removable grids, or leading. Stained glass adds soft light and a distinctive decorative touch. Order transoms, fanlights, and sidelights as a set at the same time that you order the new door.
• *Pediments*—millwork set above doors—originated in classic Greek architecture and make popular additions to more formal traditional-style homes. Unlike sidelights and transoms, a pediment is purely decorative; it may be added after the new door is installed.
• *Pilasters* are columnlike adornments used to flank an entry. In place under a pediment, a pair of pilasters will lend dignity to period architecture. Like pediments, they can

be added to an existing doorway, since no structural work is involved.
• *Hardware,* from massive knobs, handles, and ornamental escutcheon plates to wrought-iron hinges and knockers, further defines a style and accents an entry. Hardware to complement just about any style is available in a wide range of materials and finishes. (See pages 96 and 97 for more about hardware.)
• *Entry lamps* also highlight an exterior door treatment, but don't let them steal the show with overstatement. It takes a massive door and a large house to carry off an elaborate set of lanterns.

Interior doors
To a lesser but still important degree, interior doors carry out the motif of a home and complement a chosen decor. A flush door used inside a colonial house, for example, may detract from the architectural style. Even though it's likely to be less expensive than the more appropriate paneled door, the loss in terms of visual harmony may outweigh the one-time saving.

Like exterior doors, interior doors can be customized with hardware and woodwork, such as the gracefully curved door handle and traditional casing shown *below*.

INTERIOR DOOR TRIM

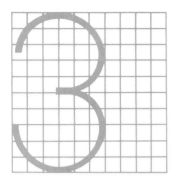

TREAT YOUR WINDOWS

For years, the only acceptable window treatments were curtains and draperies. Then, slowly, other window coverings started to make occasional appearances. Now, nearly anything goes! From flat fabric panels to folding screens, from shutters and shades to little ruffled valances, window treatments can be anything you want to use at your window—anything that controls light, provides privacy, or turns that framed-glass area into a design element.

WITH DRAPERIES

Draperies aren't only an attractive cover-up. Like other good window treatments, they can do a number of decorating jobs.

For appearance' sake
Fabric window coverings are often the surest and simplest choice when you're trying to soften the hard angles of a room's architecture. Softly pleated draperies, for example, help to tone down the severe planes of walls, floor, and ceiling.

Draperies also can alter the visual dimensions of the windows they're treating. Their style and placement can make windows appear wider, taller, or more dramatic than they actually are. In a room with tiny windows, oversize draperies create the illusion of more spacious window areas. Conversely, neatly tailored, compact draperies can change the look of overly large windows, cutting down their size to the eye without causing them to look severe.

In addition, draperies are often the answer to treating mismatched windows, which are especially common in older houses. By using draperies identical in size and style, you can blend window shapes and sizes and establish an impression of uniformity.

Placement pointers
If your house has good-looking woodwork, hang draperies inside the casing, as shown in the handsome living room *at right*. Be aware, however, that the window glass will remain partially covered at all times. To get full exposure, mount draperies well beyond the window frame; that way you can stack fabric on each side of the glass.

WITH CURTAINS

Curtains are generally considered lighter and more informal window coverings than draperies. But that's not to say they're less elegant, less charming, or even less substantial. Shown *at right* and *opposite* are curtain treatments that span the spectrum—from gauzy lace to no-nonsense, natural fabric that frames semitranslucent shades.

For practicality, it's hard to beat old-fashioned curtains. They're easy to sew, to hang, and, providing the fabric is washable, to keep clean without dry cleaning.

Curtain construction
Curtains are unlined window coverings that do not have pleated headings, as draperies do. They are flat panels with casings that gather onto rods or, in the case of cafe curtains, with top edges that feature

rings slipped onto curtain rods. Curtains hung from rings and rods allow you to slide them open and closed. However, curtains gathered onto rods are usually more stationary; often, they're tied back. In this case, you can use a second functioning window covering—shades or blinds— under the tied-back curtains.

The gathering
Although curtains are usually gathered onto standard rods

that fit snugly against the wall surface, they create an entirely different effect when gathered onto wooden cafe poles with decorative finials. When you gather a curtain panel, a ruffle automatically forms at the top edge. If you want a more pronounced ruffle, like the one shown *above,* place the rod pocket, or casing, farther from the top folded edge of the curtain or valance panel. The more space between the top edge and the casing, the

deeper and more dramatic the ruffle above the rod.

With this ring
Attach cafe curtain rings to any flat fabric panel, and you have an instant curtain. With wooden cafe rings stitched to one edge, the lace tablecloths shown *opposite* make elegant curtains. Other kinds of rings clip onto fabric, making installation even faster. See page 79 for more information about curtain rings.

37

WITH VALANCES AND SWAGS

Traditionalists may compare swags and valances to the cherry on top of a sundae — nice, but unnecessary, trimming. And it's true: These two "top treatments" often are used as decorative extras for curtains and draperies. Nevertheless, they perform equally well in solo roles. These window designs require minimal amounts of fabric, making them perfect easy-on-the-budget designs for adding that final decorating touch to a room.

The window niche *opposite* sports a ruffled valance that may appear to be too simple a window covering for a traditional room. Yet with the fabric matching the sofa cushions, this slip of a window treatment coordinates the room's decor and, at the same time, gives the plants a healthy amount of sunshine.

• A *valance* can feature a pleated heading—and look like a very short drapery—or it can be a short, flat panel curtain gathered onto a curtain rod. To make a flat valance, seam fabric widths into a panel two or three times the width of the window. Make double 1-inch hems on the sides and a double 3-inch hem on the bottom edge. For the top, turn under a ¼-inch hem on the cut edge and stitch in place. Then turn under 2¾ inches and stitch. Sew another row of stitches 1 inch from the folded bottom edge of the hem to form the pocket for the curtain rod.

• *Swags*, like the one *above*, can be draped over a cafe rod or stapled to a wooden board mounted over the window. Cut swag fabric in trapezoid shape, with top edge smaller than bottom edge. Gather at both ends.

• *Jabots* (pronounced zha-BO), or side panels, are cut with bottom edges that slant diagonally and are gathered or folded at the top edges. Attach them directly to the mounting board, with the swag over the top, or sew them to the gathered sides of the swag and drape over a cafe curtain rod.

For extra interest, line jabots with contrasting fabric, and add fabric rosettes, as shown *above*. Choose casual fabric for this cottage effect; more elegant fabric for a formal room.

TREAT YOUR WINDOWS
WITH FABRIC PANELS

Take a little fabric, add a hem to the edges, and you can create impressive fabric panels to cover any number of window shapes. Place them over just the window, or sheath the whole wall. Make them as sedate or flamboyant as the fabric you choose. And consider their purpose. There are several ways to engineer flat panels so they function as fully operable window coverings.

The two rooms that are shown here prove you don't need yards of material to create window designs that are imaginative, attractive, and practical. In both cases, flat panels dress the windows with a refreshing simplicity.

Why flat panels?
In some cases, using flat panels is an economy measure. In other instances, the fabric has so much eye-appeal that it would be senseless to hide its pattern in the folds of draperies or curtains. A better choice is to spotlight the fabric in panel window coverings, the same way you'd hang a tapestry on a wall as a focal point.

Flat panel window coverings provide one more practical advantage: a space-saving, uncluttered look that's made-to-order for contemporary life-styles.

On the right track
Sliding track systems are the key to the movable panel window treatment *above*. Here, floor-length panels hang from the ceiling-mounted track. When closed, these bold, contemporary fabric panels provide an interesting visual treatment, an effect that helps to unify a room cut up by too many doors and windows.

Pegs and dowels
In a corner where conservative colors and nubby tweeds prevail, the window treatment should reflect the same casual look. The three windows *at right* are perfectly dressed with flat panels hung from wooden dowels. Pegs, attached to the window casing, support the top and bottom dowels. To raise the panels, lift the bottom dowels to the top set of pegs.

To create this simple window design, machine-stitch side hems and pockets for the dowel rods at the top and bottom edges of each panel.

WITH SHADES

Once, the only shades you'd see were standard white or off-white rollers. They were functional but not particularly fashionable. Now everything's changed. Shades come in any number of varied designs. Even those basic rollers are available today in a wide range of colors and textures.

Which do you prefer? The trim, tailored look of horizontal folds? Or the graceful sweep of gentle poufs? You'll find well-designed shades to satisfy either choice.

Roman shades
Roman shades operate with a series of tapes and cords that lower them or draw them up. They're also extraordinarily versatile: A window treatment that requires less fabric than any other, Romans can be mounted inside or outside a window casing and can be engineered to pull from the bottom to the top of a window,

as well as designed to work in the conventional top-to-bottom arrangement.

In the dining alcove *opposite,* Roman shades of white fabric are banded with yellow accents and topped with a flat panel valance for an extra touch of color.

Austrian shades
If you like your lines a little softer than the folds of Roman shades, you may want Austrian shades, shown *above, left.* Like Roman shades, Austrian shades draw up or down by way of a series of tapes and cords. Their width, however, has to be greater than that of

Roman shades—wider than the window, in other words—to create the soft swag effect between vertical tapes. Here, the shade is mounted inside the window casing, but it can be installed with equal success outside the casing.

Balloon shades
Balloon shades, like the pretty print window covering *above, right,* are spin-offs of the Roman shade. But instead of pulling up in even, flat folds, this shade poufs up in soft flounces. Here, it's gathered onto a tension rod and installed inside the window casing.

TREAT YOUR WINDOWS

WITH WOVEN WOODS AND FABRIC SHADES

At first glance, both woven woods and fabric shades seem like workhorse window treatments you don't have to worry much about. And once you've picked the right one for your room, that's true. Making the correct choice, however, is a challenge. Woven woods come in at least four different types, ranging from simple roller shades to cafe curtains. Fabric shades offer even more design choices, in colors, textures, and decorative bottom edges, as well as the custom touches you can add once you have them home.

Woven woods, a natural choice for energy-wise home decorators, are long strips of wood held together with decorative vertical yarns. Design choices include the Roman fold, like those *opposite;* pulley styles that roll up from the bottom; spring roller shades; and short or long cafe curtains with vertical slats.

Measuring and mounting

Install woven woods either inside or outside the window opening. For inside installation, measure the width of the window opening and subtract ½ inch. All outside installations should overlap the width and length of the opening by at least 3 inches. If you are buying ready-mades instead of custom-ordering, trim wood or bamboo shades by cutting equal amounts off each side.

Plain or fancy fabric shades

Although operating any fabric roller shade is simple, you do have a variety of options that can alter the look of this popular window covering: Mount shades inside or outside the casing, order reverse-roller shades so you don't see the rollers when installed, mount them "bottoms up," or customize them with your choice of decorative trims.

Other design options: Stencil a design on the shade, use self-adhesive tape to band it, or appliqué a fabric design using white glue. If you like, make a roller shade of your own fabric, like the one *at right.* Seal the shade's edges by applying white glue to the fabric before cutting.

To order roller shades, measure the exact distance between points where the brackets will be placed, and specify whether they'll be mounted inside or outside.

WITH SCREENS

Vaudeville's quick-change artists used screens for discarding old costumes and donning new ones, all in the wink of an eye. Today's screens can perform decorating legerdemain at your windows. Install folding screens or panels that glide on a ceiling track. Cover just a portion of your window or a whole wall. Use screens as solo acts, or combine them with other window coverings.

There are plenty of reasons for screening a window area besides the architectural quality this design lends to your room.

The shoji screens *opposite*, for example, cover patio doors and, at the same time, create extra storage space. Slide the two center screens aside (there's a fourth screen off-camera) and the doors are accessible for light, air, and entry. These translucent shojis slide on a track and have soft lighting behind them. Storage shelves stand on each side of the window, and although they're easily accessible—simply by moving the panels—they're also out of sight.

Portability plus

Few window treatments are as adaptable as folding screens. Whether you use a pair of them to flank a window or a series of hinged panels to mask a portion of the window, this kind of screen folds up and travels easily from place to place.

To blend a screen treatment into the rest of the room, note the finish on the surrounding wall, and apply the same finish to the screen. You also can use a screen as an accent, painting it a contrasting color or giving it a natural wood finish. It's even possible to turn one into your room's focal point by using highly decorative panels or ornately carved screens.

A screen also may be the solution to hiding an unsightly radiator beneath the window in an older home or to shielding your view of a busy street or alley. Use a low folding screen, like the one *at left,* and combine it with a complementary window covering—cafe curtains, a woven wood shade, or venetian blinds.

WITH VENETIAN BLINDS AND VERTICAL LOUVERS

Nonfabric window treatments can give you all the color and texture of fabrics, but with a clean crisp look not generally associated with traditional fabric window coverings. Among the big favorites in nonfabric window designs are venetian blinds and vertical louvers. Both allow you to control the light entering a room and, by extension, keep the outside world from looking in.

Venetian blinds and louvers come in dozens of different colors and patterns. Even more practically, they can help lower your cooling bills. By reflecting the sun's rays, they're energy-wise window coverings that can be used in any setting.

Venetians
Choose blinds in 1- or 2-inch-wide slats, and install them either inside the window casing, or outside across the front of the window frame. Because they're generally custom-ordered, you'll have to measure carefully.

Always use a metal or wood rule. To determine width when you're working inside the casing, measure the distance—to the nearest 1/8 inch—between the inside edges of the window frame. Use this number to order the blinds; the factory will then make the slats and bottom rail slightly narrower, so they fit inside the window

frame without rubbing. To figure length, measure from the inside top edge of the casing to the top of the windowsill. If you're working outside, measure between the points where the brackets will be mounted. Once they arrive, installation will be simple. Each blind comes with brackets, screws, and mounting instructions.

Even if your room has a traditional design, you still can enjoy a contemporary, mini-slat blind window treatment. The dining room *above* successfully combines old and new.

Verticals
Vertical louvers are a streamlining window treatment that can cover a multitude of architectural flaws. The stylish louvers *at right* hang from a ceiling track and barely skim the floor. You can order vertical louvers with a decorative valance that is designed to hide the ceiling track.

WITH SHUTTERS

Shutters have been doing a good job for a long time as exterior window coverings to keep out wind and rain. Somewhere along the line, they also moved inside and since have become popular window treatments where control of light, privacy, and ventilation is important. Moreover, they have a characteristic charm that's often just the right mood-setter for an entire room scheme.

In the past, most shutters looked about the same. Today, your choices are wide open. Select from unpainted shutters you finish yourself, presanded shutters you paint or stain, and prestained shutters you simply wax or varnish. You'll also find stationary-louver shutters, movable louvers, and decorative insert frames in which you mount plastic, glass, laminate, mesh, or fabric on sash rods. Some shutters have horizontal louvers, like those shown *above;* others have vertical louvers, similar to those installed in the room *opposite.*

Measuring up

To get the right size, divide the width of the area to be covered by the number of panels you want. For instance, four panels in a 28-inch space will require 7-inch panels. Order either the exact size or the next larger size, trimming the panels to fit. Panels also may be of unequal widths. A 30-inch area, for example, could take two 7-inch and two 8-inch panels.

Hardware and hanging

Let the dealer know if you plan to mount the shutters inside or outside the window casing, so you purchase the right hard-

ware. Some shutters are sold in sets with mounting strips. Others have hanging-strip kits to make installation easier.

When you're marking spots before drilling the holes for hinges or hanging strips, rest the shutter on a coin. This will allow enough room to prevent the shutter from rubbing against the windowsill once it's installed.

WITH DECORATIVE GLASS

Decorative glass made its first great appearance in the cathedrals of the Middle Ages. Since then, it has adorned castles and manor houses, shimmered at windows and doors of Victorian homes, and decorated lamps during the Art Nouveau period. Today, using decorative glass is still an appealing way to make your windows shine.

You probably won't be lucky enough to find an old window that fits inside an existing frame. One alternative is to engineer an old glass panel to fit over or in front of a window. Another is to have a decorative glass panel custom created and installed inside your window frame.

Adapting old glass
An old stained, etched, or beveled glass panel makes a breathtaking treatment when hung over an existing window. In the room *opposite*, the glass panel is bordered by plywood frames to adapt it to the larger-size window opening. The framing structure itself is attached to the top edge of the window frame with hinges.

Glass to order
With the current interest in stained glass, you should be able to find an artisan who can design and create a window to meet all your specifications— size, color, and design motif. The stained-glass windows in the kitchen *above* were made in just that way. Constructed as a set of interior casements, they hide existing double-hung windows and add a second layer of glazing for greater energy efficiency.

You also can simply replace clear glass with decorative panes. To determine the size of the glass panel, measure the outside of your window frame, starting at the edges where the glazing begins. When ordering glass, allow a margin for fitting within the window frame. Subtract at least 1/8 inch from the actual space inside the frame.

WITH
A COMBINATION
OF COVERINGS

If one window treatment is good, two or more may be even better, depending on the location, size, and shape of your windows—and on your own approach to window design. Fortunately, no hard-and-fast rules dictate what goes where and with what. Your goal is to make sure any window treatment works well and looks good, and sometimes it takes more than one window covering to achieve the results you want.

Sometimes, an atypical size or shape window—or its placement in the wall—calls for special handling. Often, the solution to treating a window like this effectively is a combination of several coverings.

For looks, for function

The windows in the corner of the room *opposite* are a case in point. Because of their size, a treatment with some visual pizzazz is essential. But the treatment still has to control light and offer privacy. In this case, the solution is a combination of mini-louver venetian blinds for function and stationary tie-back panels under fabric-covered cornices to add the necessary pattern and softness. This fabric window treatment could serve equally well as a topping for woven woods, cafe curtains, roller shades, or even a second set of draperies, if they were installed on traverse rods to let them open and close.

Unifying separate treatments

A room with plenty of light is definitely an advantage. On the other hand, its windows may be overly large, oddly shaped, or awkwardly placed. If so, a combination treatment will help out. The living room *at right* has two separate window areas with a pair of distinctly different treatments—conventional draw draperies in the one below and vertical louvers in the angled window above. Their common characteristic is color. A neutral shade, used in both the fabric and the louvers, helps to unify the two window treatments. The result is effective: The coverings are visually compatible but still able to function independently.

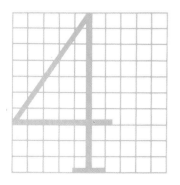

DECORATE YOUR DOORS

To many people, doors are just open-and-shut cases. Because they have to work efficiently at all times, they're sometimes short-changed in the decorating department. They may get an occasional coat of paint or varnish, but that's it. By all means, don't stop there. Door decor can be every bit the design element windows are, and to prove it, we've loaded the following pages with imaginative ideas and new looks for underdecorated doors.

A visitor's first impression of a home is often based on the way its entry looks. How does yours rate? Is it friendly? Interesting? Or just like all the others on the block?

Styling components
Depending on the character of the door and the architecture of your house, you may need more than just a good paint color. Try add-on molding, for example. Highlight details with accent colors or add sparkle with metal accents, such as knockers or mail slots.

How attractive your entry is depends largely on the area surrounding the door. If it lacks impact, think about adding shutters, bits of architecture, decorative plants, or other design elements that can help focus on the entry area and give it drama. (Pages 32 and 33 offer some architectural suggestions.)

Paint provides a practical and attractive face-lift for the entry *below*. The dark background color is sparked by contrasting hues used to edge panels and panes. (For tips on painting doors and windows, see pages 140 and 141.)

For best results, use a high-quality exterior enamel. Professionals recommend a gloss finish for doors and trim, especially with dark colors that absorb light. Gloss helps reflect the sun's rays, reducing heat absorption, which can cause the finish to crack and peel.

The back entry *opposite* has front-door importance—dazzling white paint and a spanking-new porch.

GLAMORIZE
WITH COLOR

To paint or not to paint? That is the question. When a door isn't in mint condition, but isn't worn enough to be replaced, a new coat may give it the new look it needs. Paint can cover imperfections and, at the same time, bring a touch of style to even the most ordinary door.

Color is one of those versatile tools that lets you create whatever effect you want. Used one way, it camouflages. Used another way, it lets portions of a room become colorful accents.

Crayon-box colors
Strong, pure color creates an exciting atmosphere—the perfect environment for a kid's playroom. Color is also an excellent way to decorate a wallful of closet doors. The set of old doors *opposite* is a lively start for the bands of explosive color that follow right up the sloped wall and across the ceiling. In this case, the doors are an integral part of the overall decorating scheme, instead of the oddball feature they might have been.

Although paint covers a multitude of architectural sins, it won't provide a flawless finish if you're putting it on over several previous coats. If yours is an old house with overpainted doors and trim, you'll need to strip the wood down and sand it well before applying yet another coat of paint. Remember, too, to use a paint that is highly washable so you can scrub off fingerprints.

Closeted color
A quartet of colors creates a striking door treatment in the room *above, left.* If the doors had been painted white, they would have created a large blank spot in the room's decor. Instead, four hues from the wallpaper's design appear on the door panels and frame,

helping to blend them into the color scheme.

High-velocity color
Chosen for impact, a single color can pack a mighty punch. For example, the entry *above, right* features an intense sunny yellow that brightens both the door and the entrance area. One isolated color is bound to stand out in a room, so if eye-catching attention is what you want, choose a bright color and use it boldly throughout.

Keep in mind that paint isn't the only colorful surface you can use. Try plastic laminate, or trim panel areas with vinyl wall covering. To add pattern, use paint and stencils, or apply wall covering to the panels.

LEAVE THEM NATURAL

An exterior door, like other doors and woodwork in your home, can escape the painter's brush and still look sensational. In some cases, an entry door left *au naturel* is more in keeping with the architecture of the house and a family's decorating style than a traditional painted door would be. So if you're interested in getting an old-timey look or gaining the rustic flavor of a country cottage, lock up the paint cans and leave your door the way it is.

The door shown *above* is in a style that's straight from our colonial past. This one, however, started out as an ordinary flush door in a new home. It got that centuries-old appearance from three lengths of rough-sawn cedar that had been cut to fit the existing door, then glued in place with panel adhesive.

The pegged look took a little old-fashioned whittling. The owners used 1-inch dowels, carved their ends into hexagonal shapes, and glued them into predrilled holes.

Old brass and wrought iron hardware added the final antique touches.

A natural beauty

Natural wood, weathered down to a windswept gray, has a distinctive charm. However, you can slow down the weathering process at any stage just by applying protective coats of exterior varnish. And if you're starting with a brand-new door, you can find products at paint stores that will give the door an instant weathered look.

For another version of the natural door, try the technique used on the one *opposite*. Here, old paint was stripped back to bare wood, and the wood varnished to get the rich look of accentuated grain. The painted frame around it gives the door a chance to show off its natural beauty even more.

TREAT
SLIDING GLASS
DOORS

Treat them like doors? Or treat them like windows? Sliding glass doors present special decorating problems. Whatever treatment you choose, it must allow the doors to work properly, while also controlling light and providing privacy. And because some sliding glass doors are notorious energy-wasters, your treatment also should be designed to help cut down on heat losses.

The beauty of a sliding glass door is that it's open to the outdoors. When the weather's fine and the view is scenic, looking through the sliding glass door is a splendid sight indeed. But at night or on a gloomy day, that large expanse of glass needs something more visually attractive.

Lattice dressing
Custom-made lattice panels, suspended from an overhead track, dress the sliding glass doors *opposite* and do the job

without upsetting the flow of traffic. To hide the track, the owners built a simple wooden frame with an 8-inch heading around the doors.

The same kind of frame, employed *opposite* to create lattice panels, can be used with other types of decorative grillwork, fabric, or hardboard sheets covered with vinyl.

Made in the shade
The sun-drenched family room *below* needed a treatment that could control light flooding through its sliding doors. A

series of roller shades filled the bill, each with a customizing band of grosgrain ribbon stitched along the bottom edge. A baffle, installed at the top of the sliding doors, conceals the rollers and gives a unified look to the twin shades. Tasseled, fabric bell pulls, hung from the baffle, tidy up the edges of the shades.

Treatments on sliding glass doors not only need to control light, they should also help to conserve energy. (For ideas on energy-saving window treatments, see Chapter 7.)

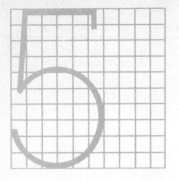

5
PLANNING WINDOW TREATMENTS

There's more to choosing a window dressing than just covering the glass. Sometimes budget dictates a treatment; sometimes it's the unique shape or size of the window. The deciding factor might be energy conservation, the demands of a particular living situation, or visual appeal. To introduce you to some of the main considerations, we visited five homes, queried their owners about needs and wants, then designed and executed solutions. The results appear on the next ten pages. In the remainder of the chapter, we show you how to analyze and measure the windows at your house and choose the best treatments for them.

BAY WINDOWS

"We never seem to stay in one place more than a few years. Just about the time we feel settled into a house, a transfer comes along, and we pack up and move again.

"This is the first house we've lived in that's had a bay window—and I love it. But I'm not sure the next house we move to will have the same kind of windows."

Flexibility was first on this family's list of requirements, so we steered them away from an expensive custom window treatment that might not be appropriate for their next home.

Ready-made ruffled curtains give a homey look at a price that won't strain the family budget. For maximum versatility, we chose a soft go-with-everything color and decided to treat each window of the bay as a separate unit. This way the curtains have a good chance of working well somewhere in the family's next house.

To unify the treatment we used a curtain rod specially designed for bay windows; its center support keeps the rod from sagging. As a final touch we placed the tiebacks where the window sashes meet, giving the bay a nice clean line and the traditional tiebacks a fresher look.

Ready-made curtains in a classic style are a good choice for families on the move, who need to get a lot of mileage out of a window treatment. Page 74 offers other decorating options for bay windows.

SINGLE WINDOWS

A single window lets in light, may open onto a view you'd ordinarily miss, and can break up a potentially monotonous wall. But it also poses some decorating problems. How do you make a single window blend with other, possibly larger, windows on other walls of the room? How can you make it work with the walls and furnishings if it's the only window on the wall—or in the whole room? How can it be the decorating plus that all windows should be? On these two pages and on page 75, we'll show you how to conquer single windows almost single-handedly.

"We're still living in our first little home in the suburbs—we've been here for six years. It's a small builder's house and there's certainly nothing wrong with it, but everything seems pretty ordinary. What we're trying to do now is make it look as individual as possible.

"The single window in the living room was just an opening in the middle of the end wall. We wanted to figure out a way to take advantage of the light and ventilation it could provide, yet make the window look bigger and more important—maybe with a little of the architectural flair that the house itself lacks."

The cozily elegant room *opposite* is the happy result of the homeowners' meeting with our designers.

Shutters seemed like a good place to start. They cover not only the window but also the previously blank space between the windowsill and the floor. The shutters used here are a little larger than the window, since precisely fitted shutter panels weren't available.

To make the window look bigger, we built a wooden frame to surround the window and attached it to the wall to support the shutters. The shutters are hinged to each other and open to one side. Adjustable louvers allow the shutters to let in light or provide full privacy.

Stretching with fabric

Once the shutters were established as attractive and functional window treatments, we added neutral but darker-toned curtain panels on either side of the shutters, which expanded the size of the window horizontally as well as vertically. The wooden cafe pole and brackets sustain the warm look of the shutters.

Instead of the usual wooden rings, we hung the curtains directly on the rod. Each homemade curtain is simply a flat panel of fabric with a pocket for the cafe pole to go through—an easy evening's sewing project.

For added emphasis, the remainder of the cafe pole is covered with curtain fabric. This "custom" detail is just a long sleeve with a top hem the same size as the one on the curtains. It's gathered onto the rod between the two curtain panels, so the top ruffle goes all the way across the window.

Achieve a similar but softer effect by replacing the shutters with a fabric treatment such as cafe curtains or Roman shades to match or coordinate with the floor-length curtains.

The components of this simple but effective single-window project are shown *above*. All are widely available at home centers and fabric stores.

PLANNING WINDOW TREATMENTS

CORNER WINDOWS

Corner windows provide twice the light and twice the view of a single window, but decorating them calls for more than merely doubling a single window treatment. In a corner, you'll often find two windows placed so they meet head-on, leaving no room for separate, side-by-side treatments. If this is the case, decorate the windows as a single unit. Be especially careful when choosing and positioning hardware. If you opt for draperies, each window should have its own one-way-draw traverse rod so the fabric will stack at the outer edge of each window. Mount slat blinds and shades so they can move freely without interfering with each other. For more ideas about how to avoid getting backed into a corner with corner window treatments, see page 75.

"What we really wanted was to leave our windows bare—no covering at all. We like the openness and the light. When we married and bought this house, we didn't want to decorate it with fancy, uncomfortable furniture and yards of window fabric blocking both the view outside and the light coming in. That's how we felt. And I guess we still do. But we had to give up the idea of nothing at all on the windows.

"This room is our den and guest room, and its corner windows face southwest. Much as we liked the view, we needed something to control the light—and the heat."

Our designers suggested mini-slat blinds to provide temperature and light control without sacrificing the view. The blinds' sleek, uncluttered styling suited the couple's taste, and the slats are practically invisible when they're angled just the right way.

For added ease of operation, the blinds were ordered to fit inside the window frame. The top bracket, which is the same color as the blinds, fits up under the frame to give the window a neat, tailored look.

Both window blinds have their cords and wands on the outside edge so they're easy to reach. As you can see from the samples *at right*, mini-slats come in a wide range of colors to complement any decor.

Are our "clients" happy with their new mini-slat treatment? "Considering we had some very definite ideas about what we *didn't* want at our windows, it didn't take us long to see how practical this window covering would be for us. And it's probably the next best thing to no window treatment at all."

MULTIPLE WINDOWS

Two, three, or more windows placed side by side in a wall offer plenty of decorating options. You can treat each window to a separate covering, or handle the series as one design element with a single unifying treatment. With this much glass area, your windows can be the focal point of all or part of a room. The only drawback to a bank of windows is that it can be expensive to decorate. On these two pages and on page 76, we'll show you how to make the most of many windows, without necessarily spending a lot to do it.

"After years of renting, I decided to buy a house. I wasn't fully prepared for the expenses that hit me all at once, and they left me with very little extra to spend on niceties such as special window treatments."

Some kind of window covering was needed right away in this single homeowner's bedroom, where a pair of side-by-side windows provided no privacy. Our team agreed with her that an attractive, practical, and economical window treatment was an immediate necessity.

The blue balloon shades *opposite* were the perfect answer. They add a welcome softness and bright color in an otherwise tailored home, and they were easy to make. These required only 7 yards of material; conventional draperies would have taken 12 yards—24 yards if lined. The cost of the fabric, notions, and hardware for these balloon shades was slightly over half the cost of homemade lined draperies.

As you can see from the components *at right*, it doesn't take a lot of anything to put balloon shades together—just fabric, Roman shade tape, loops, cord, a spring rod, and a wooden dowel to go at the bottom of the balloons. Detailed instructions for making balloon shades and other related treatments, such as Roman shades, are widely available in decorating and sewing publications.

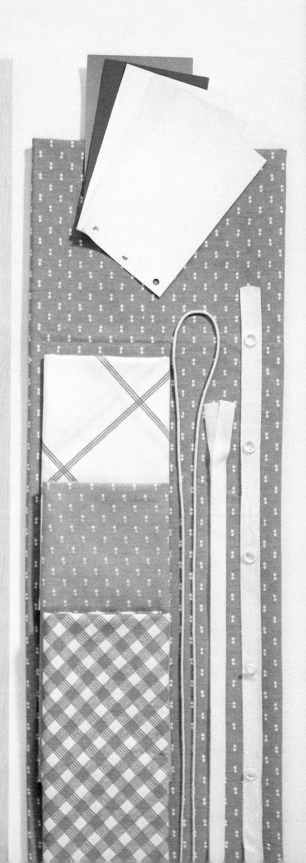

SLIDING GLASS DOORS

Few window treatments are tougher to plan than those for sliding glass doors. The problem, of course, is that they *are* doors, and any treatment you choose must allow them to open and close freely. At the same time, the expanse of glass demands that they be treated like windows—with a covering to enhance them and provide privacy and light control. Because glass is a poor insulator, choose a sliding-door treatment with energy efficiency in mind. Woven woods and lined fabric draperies are naturals here; for other decorative solutions to the sliding-door puzzle, see page 76.

"One of the reasons we bought our house was this family room and deck. The deck is a great place for our two small children to play. It keeps them nearby, and the sliding doors are easy for them to open and close. But as the utility bills started coming in, we realized that there are some disadvantages to sliding glass doors."

When it came to investing in a window treatment for the family room, saving energy was high on the list of priorities. The family wanted to block the heat of the afternoon sun in summer and provide a barrier against the cold in winter. They also wanted privacy from the neighbors.

"We thought this was a tall order to fill, until the designers from *Better Homes and Gardens*® suggested woven woods. We had thought that an energy-saving window treatment meant hoisting a heavy shade up and down, and we were pleasantly surprised to discover that woven woods could be mounted from a heading system so they operate like draperies."

Wood is a good natural insulator, especially when teamed with tightly woven yarn—the more yarn the better. The samples *at right* are in neutral tones, but woven woods with brightly colored yarns also are available.

Although woven wood draperies are available with their own matching headers, we added a wooden cornice above the doors to conceal fluorescent tube lighting and give the treatment an architectural look. The cornice acts as an additional energy-saver by blocking drafts at the top of the window. (For more about energy-efficient window treatments, see Chapter 7.)

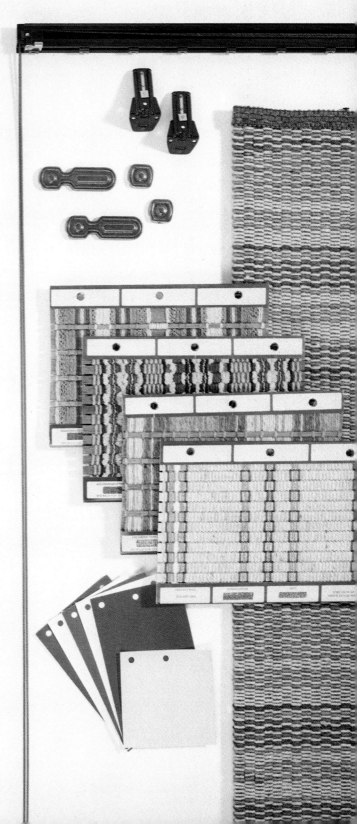

WINDOW STYLING SKETCHBOOK

Although most windows are basically the same shape, the ways they're arranged and how they open and close vary quite a bit. It's these variations that determine which window treatments will look and function best on a particular window. On the next four pages, we've put together a sketchbook of seven of the most common window configurations and treated each in six different ways. Use our sketches to help plan the best design for *your* windows.

Planning a window treatment involves a series of logical steps. First, determine just what you want your window covering to do—control light, provide privacy, save energy, serve as a major design element in your room, or accomplish some, all, or none of these.

Next, analyze the window itself. Is it too large? Too small? Awkwardly placed? Or just right? Does it open in an unusual way that requires a special treatment?

Once you've answered these questions, you're on the way to choosing a window treatment. For example, if you think a window is too small and you'd like it to look bigger, perhaps a floor-to-ceiling covering is the answer. If you're dealing with "windows" that are really sliding glass doors or French doors, think in terms of a window treatment that won't get in the way of the doors opening and closing.

A last step in planning a window treatment is to look at your budget. If funds are limited, look to a fabric-saving treatment, such as Roman or balloon shades, inexpensive ready-made curtains, decorative roller shades, or matchstick blinds. Which one of these you choose will depend on the window's main function—light, air, privacy, or decoration—as well as your taste.

Once you've reviewed your windows, what they do and how they do it, you can choose the best design. Study the ideas shown *at right* and *opposite,* and browse through window decorating books and magazines, drapery hardware brochures, and local stores' drapery departments. You'll soon have more ideas to use than windows to use them on.

BAY WINDOWS

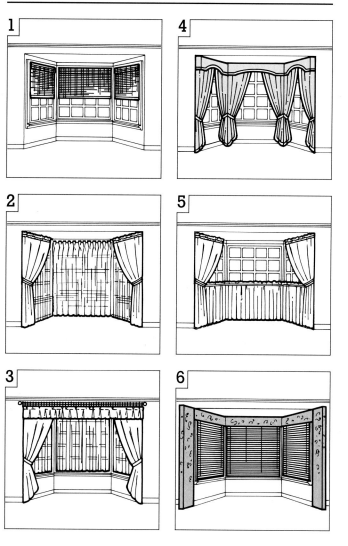

Here are six ideas that work well for bays.

1. Mount woven wood blinds within the window frame of each window of the bay.

2. Hang floor-length tie-back curtains at the sides of the bay, with sheers hung from a custom-ordered angled rod that spans the bay.

3. Try stationary tiebacks at sides of the bay, with valance across the top and sheer curtains covering each window.

4. For a formal look, use floor-to-ceiling draperies at each window. Unify the area with a sculptured cornice.

5. To make a small bay seem larger, mount a rod halfway between the ceiling and the floor and use to-the-floor curtains. Add stationary tiebacks at sides of the bay.

6. Treat each window to a mini-slat blind, then emphasize the area with a wood lambrequin, or frame.

SINGLE WINDOWS

CORNER WINDOWS

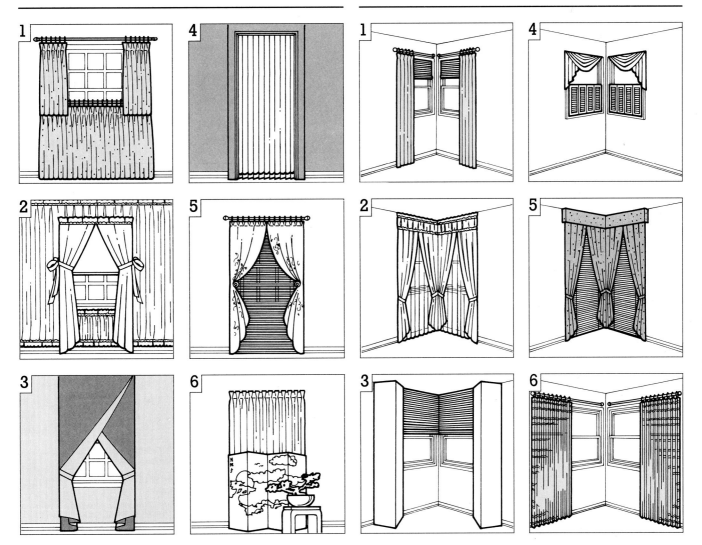

Usually, the secret to treating a single window right is to make it look bigger than it is.

1. Hang two tiers of cafe curtains on rods mounted on wall outside window frame. Extend bottom tier to the floor.

2. Tie back floor-length draperies that match or coordiate with the fabric covering the walls. Use a window shade for privacy and light control.

3. Hang two flat fabric panels from double curtain rods, one in front of the other. Fold back to expose the lining.

4. Give a single window impact with floor-length, vertical louver blinds surrounded by a lambrequin.

5. Top floor-length mini-slat blinds with traverse draperies caught on holdbacks.

6. Hide an air conditioner with a four-panel screen. Cover the rest of the window with draperies that fall just below the screen's top edge.

Give each window a separate treatment, but aim for the effect of a single design.

1. Hang two panels of floor-length draperies from separate one-way traverse rods, or use cafe rods and rings. Mount shades inside frames.

2. Mount two sets of double curtain rods above each window, one over the casing, the other 8 inches above. The flat valance panel goes on the outer rods, the tiebacks and the

sheers on the inner rods.

3. Flank ceiling-high Roman shades with floor-to-ceiling bi-fold panels.

4. Shutter lower half of windows and top them with swags and jabots.

5. Top floor-length mini-slats with tie-back draperies and a ceiling-high cornice.

6. Use woven woods as draperies. Install heavy-duty rods to support the weight.

(continued)

WINDOW STYLING SKETCHBOOK
(continued)

A SERIES OF WINDOWS

SLIDING GLASS

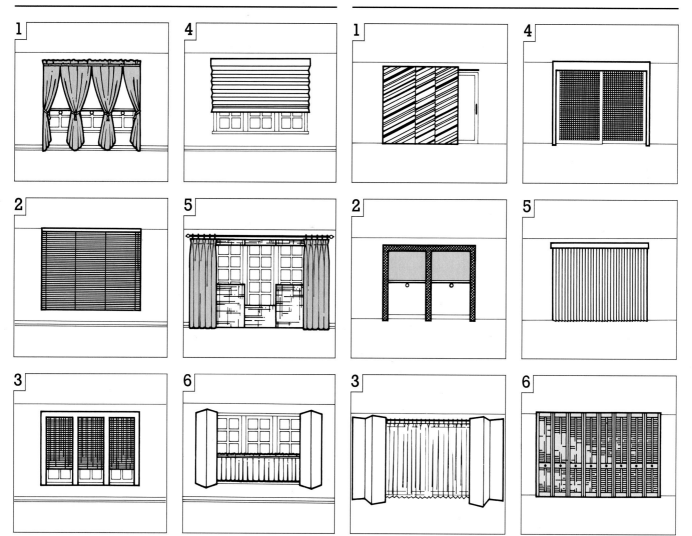

A series of windows can be very impressive. Here are some ideas for treatments that are worthy of their size.

1. Hang floor-length tiebacks from one heavy-duty rod. Add roller shades at each window for privacy and light control.

2. Cover the entire window area with one large mini-slat blind for a streamlined look.

3. Outfit each window with individual woven wood blinds; top off with a lambrequin to hide the hardware and give the treatment an architectural look.

4. Use a single Roman shade over all the windows for dramatic impact.

5. Disguise window length with bottoms-up woven woods mounted at floor level. Add side draperies to dress it up.

6. Gather curtains onto a rod installed to cover the lower portion of the window area; flank the curtains with bifold panels or shutters.

Here are some suggestions for windows that are doors first and foremost.

1. Hang fabric panels on a special track system so they slide from one side to another.

2. Mount roller shades on the wall above the doors, then hide the rollers behind a lambrequin.

3. Use a one-way traverse rod for draperies; for added interest, bracket the draperies with folding screens.

4. Install custom-made latticework panels on an overhead track; hide the track with a lambrequin.

5. Treat the doors to vertical louvered blinds that not only turn 180 degrees for good light, but also pull to one side.

6. Try floor-to-ceiling shutters. Hinge them so half open to the left, half to the right, and all stand beside the doors when completely open.

IN-SWINGING CASEMENTS

FRENCH DOORS

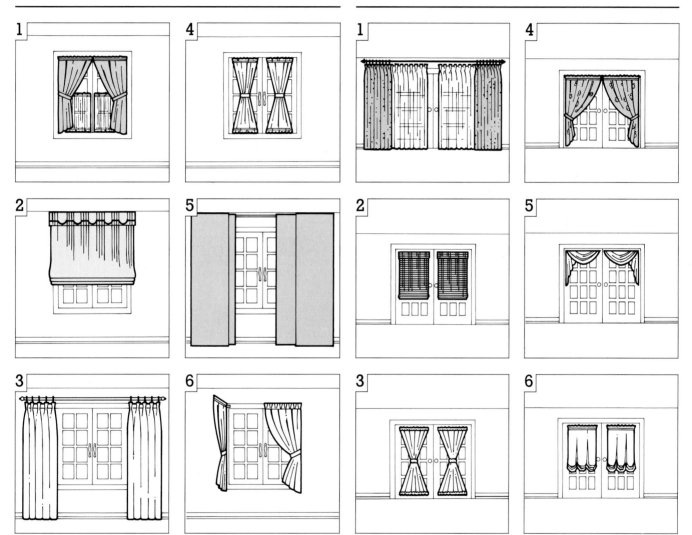

Standard casements that open out can be treated like double-hung windows. For in-swinging casements, use a treatment that won't interfere with the windows' operation.

1. Mount decorative tiebacks on each window. For privacy, add a sash curtain below.

2. Mount woven wood Roman shades at the ceiling line so they can be raised enough to let windows open easily.

3. Use traditional drapery

treatments, but extend well beyond the window frame.

4. Attach sash curtain rods to the top and bottom of each window, then add flat fabric panels, gathered cottage-style.

5. Hang floor-length sliding fabric panels from a ceiling track. Half should slide to the left, half to the right, and all stack back beside the window.

6. Mount a swinging crane rod above each window—light-weight curtains will work best.

French doors, whether single or double, are delightful, but they present decorating dilemmas that combine the problems of in-swinging casements with those of sliding glass doors. Here are some ideas for solving those problems.

1. Mount a double traverse rod well above the door. Sheers and overdraperies should stack beside the door.

2. Cover each door with a woven wood Roman shade.

Special brackets keep lower portions from swinging free.

3. Use cottage curtains, sash-mounted at the bottom and top.

4. Gather fabric panels onto curtain rods installed at the top of each door, and tie back.

5. Swags on each door with jabots on outer edges give a balanced look.

6. Balloon shades add a romantic look; make sure edges do not interfere with door.

SELECTING HARDWARE

Choosing the right hardware for your window treatments starts with buying the right rods. After that, the hooks and rings are easy. Different types of rods perform different jobs—tie-back curtains, for example, were never meant to fit onto traverse rods. And certain rods, like certain window treatments, fit better in some settings than in others. Here's an overview of the most popular standard hardware. Use it to figure out exactly what you need to make your carefully planned window treatments look their best.

Your choice of hardware depends, first of all, on whether you've chosen a stationary treatment, such as tie-back curtains, or a movable treatment, such as overdraperies and sheers. Rods for stationary window treatments are usually the simplest, since they don't have to do anything except keep the curtains in place.

Curtain rods
The rods used for stationary rod-pocketed curtains vary mainly according to where you want to mount them.

1. *Projecting curtain rods* attach to the window casing or to the walls on either side. They come in several expandable lengths and projection depths and are used for tie-backs, shirred curtains, and other treatments where the rod doesn't show. Double projecting rods are similar in design but have two projections— for example, 2½ and 3½ inches—to allow for a valance as well as curtains.

2. *Sash rods* attach directly to the sash and allow you to hang lightweight fabrics close to the window surface. They are used primarily for shirred curtains on in-swinging casement windows and French doors.

3. *Spring tension rods* fit between the two jambs of a window and are ideal for shirred curtains or locations where casing-, wall-, or sash-mounted hardware won't do.

4. *Drapery cranes* are movable hardware. They're lifesavers where you need flexible installations, particularly for in-swinging casement windows or French doors. Cranes operate on a hinged bracket that allows the free end of the rod to swing out, away from

CURTAIN RODS

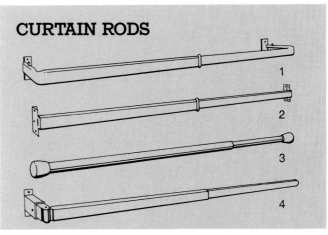

TRAVERSE RODS

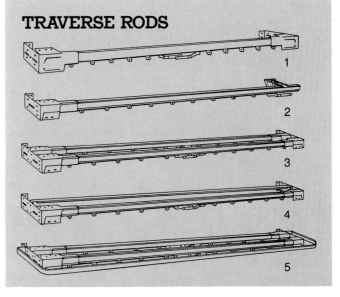

DECORATIVE RODS

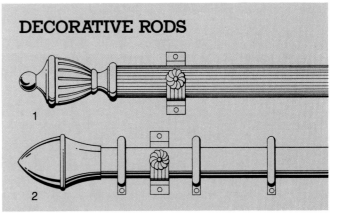

HOOKS AND RINGS

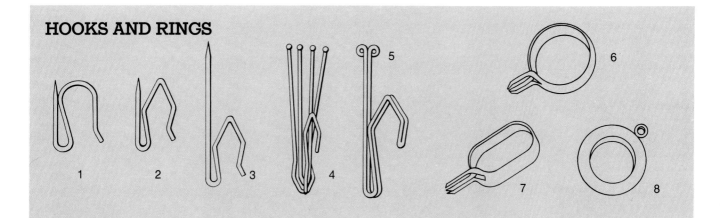

the moving door or window. The bracket can be attached to either the casing or wall.

Traverse rods

If you are planning window treatments that open and close, you'll need traverse rods. Like the stationary hardware described opposite, many traverse rods come in a plain white or off-white painted metal. They are intended to be unobtrusive, to blend with any room and add little to its decorative mood.

1. *Conventional traverse rods* are used with classic two-part pleated draperies that pull from the center to each side of the window.

2. *One-way-draw traverse rods* allow the draperies to be pulled entirely to one side of the window or the other. They're especially effective for corner windows or spaces where there is more room on one side of the window than on the other. They are available in both right- and left-hand draw.

3. *Double traverse rods* operate separately but are attached to the same mounting bracket. This system lets you hang two pairs of draperies at one window conveniently—for example, light-controlling sheers nearer the window and heavier energy-saving fabric as the next layer. Combinations of stationary and traverse rods also are available.

4. *Traverse and plain rods* let you hang draw draperies on the room side and stationary curtains closer to the window—a good system for shirred curtains with privacy-providing overdraperies.

5. *Triple rods* combine two traverse rods with a curtain rod on the room side; this means you can hang a valance—pleated or gathered—above a layered drapery treatment.

Decorative rods

Not all window treatment hardware comes with a plain, no-nonsense look. Some rods are designed to be shown off and to serve as decorative accents.

1. *Cafe curtain rods*, available in metal or wood in a variety of finishes, are used with cafe rings rather than drapery hooks. Cafe curtains are opened and closed manually instead of with cord-pulls.

2. *Decorative traverse rods* look like cafe curtain rods, but offer the cord-pull convenience of conventional traverse rods. You attach the hooks of pleated draperies into ring-like slides. These rods also come in shiny brass, antique brass, wood finishes, white, and an assortment of other metallic finishes.

Hooks and rings

Hooks and rings are the links between your window treatment and the rod that holds it up. There are several types of drapery hooks, and each is used in a different situation.

1. *Round pin-on hooks* are used when fabric treatments with closed-bottom headings (the pleats or gathers at the top of curtains and draperies) are hung from stationary rather than traverse rods.

2. *Pointed-top pin-on hooks* are used when closed-bottom treatments are hung from traverse rods. They also attach to cafe rings.

3. *Heavy-duty pin-on hooks* are used with heavy fabrics.

4. *Pleater hooks* are used with pleater tape. Each prong goes into a pocket of the tape to make the pleat.

5. *Slip-on hooks* are used for draperies with open-bottom headings. The hooks slip up under the heading and clamp around individual pleats.

6. *Clip-on cafe rings*, like these, are used with round cafe rods.

7. *Clip-on cafe rings*, like these, are used with curtain rods.

8. *Eyelet cafe rings* are used for curtains that are hung from drapery hooks and used as lightweight traverse draperies.

Buy cafe rings about ¼ inch larger than the diameter of your cafe rod to make sure curtains will slide easily. Plan three rings for every foot of rod, plus one extra ring if your cafe is a single panel, two if you have a pair of cafes at one window. If your cafes are pinch-pleated, buy a ring for every pleat.

MEASURING FOR WINDOW TREATMENTS

Once you've decided what kind of window treatments you want, it's time to do some very careful measuring. Exactly when you measure depends on whether your treatments will be custom- or ready-made. If you're buying ready-made curtains or draperies, simply find the size that matches your window area best; you'll be able to make minor fitting adjustments by moving the rod. If you're sewing your own window treatments or having them made for you, mount the hardware first. To ensure proper fit, you'll need two precise measurements—the distance between brackets and the distance from the top of the rod to wherever you want your fabric to extend. On these two pages, we'll show you how to make sure your window treatments are just the right size.

Whatever kind of window treatment you've decided on, here are some tips to ensure accurate measurements.
- Measure with a steel tape or carpenter's rule; cloth tapes can sag or stretch.
- Write down all measurements as you take them; they are easily transposed or forgotten.
- Measure every window. Particularly in older houses, windows that look the same size can vary by an inch or more.

Measuring for ready-mades
If you're planning to buy ready-made curtains or draperies, you'll have several sizes to choose from. As a rule of thumb, you'll need fabric that's at least twice as wide as the area you want to cover, but different treatments look best with varying degrees of fullness. Remember that the fabric width must include the returns at each end of the rod and, for draperies, the overlap at the center. Often, the package will tell you which size you need for a particular treatment.

Length is up to you. By adjusting the height of the rods—they'll go anywhere from the ceiling down to the casing—you can make ready-made window treatments work even for windows that aren't quite standard.

Don't spare the rod
There are four possible places to install drapery hardware: the ceiling, the wall, the casing as shown in the drawing *opposite,* and inside the casing. Rods mounted on or inside the casing are limited in size by the width of the window, but rods mounted on the wall or ceiling can extend as far as you want. Wall- or ceiling-mounted rods lend themselves to impressive and dramatic window treatments.

Wall rods are usually installed about 4 inches above the window glass; this masks the heading and hardware when viewed from outside.

When you're determining the rod's length, allow space for the draperies to stack back enough when they're open so that the glass can be completely uncovered.

To figure the total stack-back room required for a pair of draperies, divide the window glass width (in inches) by 3, and add 12 inches. Add this stack-back figure to the width of the window glass to get the total length you'll need for your rod. Then, for center-draw draperies, divide the stack-back figure in half to find how much space you need on each outer edge of the window glass. For one-way draws, of course, the entire stack back will be on one side. Extend your drapery rods accordingly.

Measuring for custom-mades
Once the rods are installed, you're ready to measure for made-to-measure draperies and curtains.
- *Width*. Measure the length of the rod from bracket to bracket. Double that measurement (or triple it for extra fullness). Add the space for the returns, plus 4 inches for center overlap. (If you use a one-way traverse rod, there's no overlap.) The total is the finished width of your draperies. The drawing *opposite* shows each dimension you need.
- *Length*. If your draperies or curtains are to be hung from nondecorative rods, measure from the top of the installed rod. Unlike curtains, whose tops are often even with the top of the rod, hook-hung draperies should extend at least ½ inch above the rod; check your hooks and add the

correct amount to the length measurement. For decorative rods, measure the length from the bottom of the rings.

Several common lengths are shown in the drawing *opposite*. Short draperies or curtains fall to the windowsill or to the top of the apron. Draperies and curtains on wall-mounted rods usually fall to the bottom of the apron or to the floor. Window treatments hung from casing-mounted rods generally extend to the windowsill or the apron. Curtains hung from rods that are mounted inside the casing should drop only to the sill.

Remember to allow floor-length draperies or curtains to clear the floor by about an inch. If you have baseboard heating, be sure the window treatment won't interfere with airflow.

Installing draperies
Once the initial measuring is done, the hardware is in place, and the treatments are ready for hanging, keep these points in mind.
- *Headings*. Nondecorative traverse rods or curtain rods place the heading level with the top of the rod. Decorative traverse rods and cafe curtain rods are visible: The top of the heading comes to the bottom of the rings.
- *Good coverage*. Make sure your curtains or draperies are full enough to cover the area you want them to.
- *Smooth sliding*. Start hanging your drapery panel at the master slide in the center of the rod. Attach a hook into each slide after that and work to the end of the rod. If the rod has more slides than you need, slip some off the end. Make sure that pleats are straight and that the space between pleats is smooth.

POINTS OF REFERENCE

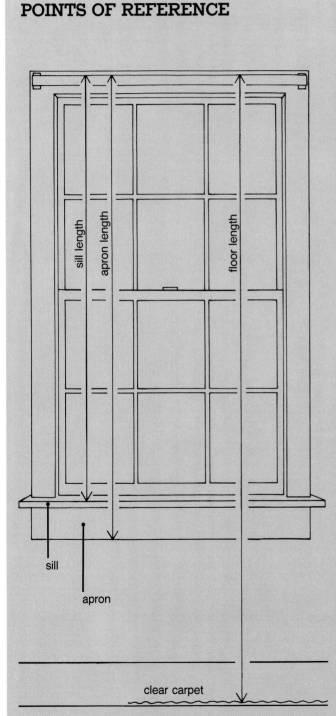

sill length

apron length

floor length

sill

apron

clear carpet

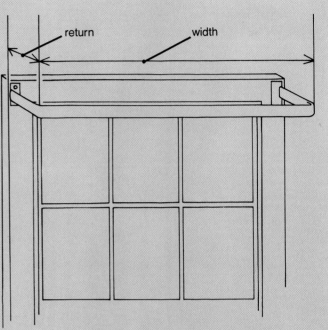

return

width

MEASURING TIPS

Here are a few specific hints to make measuring for window treatments a little easier and a lot more accurate.

• *For cafe curtains*, determine the length of each tier by measuring from the lower part of the clips or rings on the upper rod to 3 inches below the clips or rings on the lower rod. If you want the bottom rods and rings showing—and you probably will for carefully chosen decorative rods—just measure from the bottom of the rings on the top rod to the top of the lower rod.

• *For inside-mounted curtains*, measure the distance from the top of the rod to the windowsill; length here is limited by the rod's placement.

• *For shirred curtains*, measure from 1 inch above the top of the rod to the sill, apron, or floor, depending on the desired length. This allows for a 1-inch heading above the rod pocket.

• *For shades, blinds, woven woods, mini-slats, shutters, and other nonflexible treatments*, measurements have to be, if anything, more precise than the ones we've explained above. Your retailer will help you with these measurements and perhaps even send someone to your home to do the measuring for you. Required dimensions may differ from one product to another.

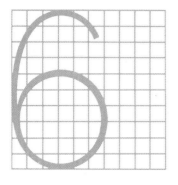

UPGRADING WINDOWS AND DOORS

Not too many years ago, style alone dictated the kinds of windows and doors used in a home. Of course, that was before the cost of heating and cooling started to soar out of sight. Today, no matter how good they look, energy-wasting doors and windows are like a hole in your pocket, especially when modern manufacturing techniques allow you to buy replacement windows and doors that are energy efficient and nearly maintenance-free. True, the cost of upgrading represents a sizable investment, so the decisions you reach must be careful ones. In this chapter, you'll find information and do-it-yourself advice to help you make the right choices.

BUYING WINDOWS

Try these tests. Open a double-hung window partway and attempt to move it from side to side. Any give means it probably leaks air. Or wait for a cold or windy day to move a fluffy feather or narrow strip of tissue slowly around the closed sash. If you see movement, your windows are letting the cold in and the heat out.

If your home was built more than 10 years ago, its windows may need replacing. Old wooden windows tend to shrink, letting air leak in, or infiltrate. A crack $\frac{1}{16}$ inch wide around a 3x5-foot window is equivalent to having a hole in one wall the size of a brick! Early aluminum windows lack the insulating qualities available today and lose heat by conduction. For the same reason, once widely used steel sliding windows are also prime candidates for replacement.

Well-constructed, modern windows can greatly reduce your heating and cooling costs. How? By bringing in warm sunlight in winter and not allowing warm air to escape. In summer, the reverse is true—cooled air is kept inside and heat is insulated out. Too, as sources for cooling breezes, windows lighten your air conditioning load.

Window shopping
The overall performance, durability, and energy efficiency of any new window depends upon its major components: glass (glazing), weather stripping, hardware, and sash and frame material.
• *Glass.* Quality windows sold today are double-glazed—two panes of glass with an insulating air space between. Double-glazing is twice as effective in reducing heat loss as a single-pane window. Triple- and even quadruple-glazing also

are available at correspondingly higher prices. In a multiple-glazed unit, look for a hermetically sealed space between panes that is at least ¾ inch thick (and no more than 1 inch thick). Exterior storm sashes (see page 86) installed over double-glazed windows will be nearly as efficient as triple-glazing.

In climates where the sun's heat poses a problem, tinted or reflective glass can reduce solar gain, yet still provide plenty of light. Clear and tinted acrylic plastic is often used as glazing material. In addition, there are intriguing design variations that incorporate venetian-type blinds into the air space between panes.
• *Weather stripping.* Cracks and crevices around a window's perimeter allow outside air to leak in. To seal out drafts, windows should have efficient weather stripping built in at the factory. Good weather stripping is flexible and compresses tightly when the unit is closed, to keep infiltration to a minimum.
• *Hardware.* Hardware should be of high quality. Locks must be sturdy and close the window tightly. Operating mechanisms of hardened steel (on casement and crankable types) are best. The opening and closing of any window should be quiet and effortless, without jamming or sticking.
• *Sash and frame material.* Wood and aluminum are the most common framing materials, and each has its merits. Wood does not conduct heat; aluminum readily does. Wood, however, requires periodic painting, while aluminum is practically maintenance-free. Wood frames may eventually

shrink and leak air. Aluminum won't shrink, but components may not fit tightly to begin with.

Nevertheless, manufacturers have effectively dealt with all these drawbacks. Today, you'll find wood frames with aluminum or vinyl on the outside to resist weathering. Contemporary aluminum windows often include a thermal break, which is a strip of vinyl or polymer inserted between the sashes and frame to keep air from passing between components.

Joints in any window unit should be tight. Wood joints should be mortised and tenoned, and secured with waterproof glue as well as nails or screws. Aluminum window joints should be lapped and continuous-welded.

Rating energy efficiency

All windows carry two ratings that define energy efficiency. One is called a U-value, and is to windows what R-value is to insulation. A U-value is a measure of heat flow through a given material. Specifically, it shows the amount of heat a window allows to escape per hour. You'll usually find two values quoted—one for the glass and one for the window as a whole. In both cases, lower ratings mean greater energy efficiency.

The other rating is R-value—a measurement of the glazing's resistance to heat passing through it. With R-values, the higher the number, the better the unit's heat resistance. A single-glazed window has an R-value of about 1. Double-glazing rates about 1.8; triple-glazing, approximately 2.7.

Because all newly manufactured windows have both U- and R-values, use them as guides when you shop for replacement units.

INSTALLING NEW WINDOWS

New windows are not only an energy-saving investment, they also enhance an older home's appearance and boost its resale value. Plus, setting in new windows isn't as complicated as you might think.

Start by evaluating your existing windows. Often, because they're in the wrong place to begin with, it's a good idea to replace *and* relocate them at the same time.

What's a window to do?

So they'll be most energy efficient, place windows where they can take greatest advantage of the sun's heat and light and where you can open them for natural cross ventilation. Here are some tips to keep in mind:

• *For the most light*, use one large window, rather than several small ones. To get even light throughout the room, use windows in more than one wall. Tall windows let light farther into the room than short, wide ones.

• *For the most ventilation*, the size of window openings should equal at least 10 percent of each room's floor area. Windows on opposite walls are best; adjacent walls, next best. Keep them out of corners. Window styles also determine how much they can be opened to admit breezes.

• *For the most energy savings*, keep the sun in mind. Where winters are cold, the largest window areas should face south to take advantage of solar gain. The smallest amount of glass should be on the north side. Where air conditioning costs are a prime concern, the largest window area should be to the north and the smallest to the west and south.

Getting started

Window units come preassembled. All you have to do is build the "rough" opening, tip the unit into place, then add trim around the edges. If it all sounds too simple, remember that there is quite a bit of preparation before you can set any new window into place. (Of course, if you're just replacing a window, you'll already have the rough opening once you remove the old sash and frame.)

Plan carefully before cutting into a wall. Decide exactly where you want the window, then determine if there are any plumbing pipes, heating ducts, or electrical wires in that spot. You can easily relocate wiring, but not plumbing or heating.

Your supplier will give you the rough-in dimensions for the window unit. The exterior opening will need to be only slightly larger. On the inside, the wall surface from ceiling to floor must be removed within the rough-in dimensions. Cut from the inner edge of the first stud past either side of the measurement. Working from the inside out, you'll cut through the exterior sheathing and siding just before you insert the window. The step-by-step procedure shown on these pages will help you complete your project.

Keep two things in mind when installing a window: Framing for the rough opening must be strong and accurate; and everything must be plumb, level, and square, or the window won't work correctly.

SETTING NEW WINDOWS

1 Mark the interior dimensions on the wall. Remove the baseboard with a flat pry bar, pulling nails through the back. Find studs by driving a nail through the spot where the baseboard was fastened. To find wiring, cut very carefully around wall outlets. If no wires are present, cut the drywall with a keyhole saw, ceiling to floor (not through the soleplate), to the inside of the studs on your rough-in dimensions.

2 Remove the section of drywall. Take out the insulation between studs, then cut and remove sections of the exposed studs that will be interrupted by the window. Pry stud pieces carefully away from the sheathing.

3 To start construction of the rough opening framing, build a header. Sandwich a scrap of ½-inch plywood between two 2x6s (or 2x12s as shown) cut to fit between the studs. Position the header snugly under the top plate and toenail it to the studs. Cut a 2x4 sill to fit between studs and two 2x4s to go from soleplate to sill. Nail 2x4s to the bottom of the sill at each end. Insert the sill in place and finish nailing in.

4 Cut three 2x4s to go from sill to header. Nail one to the stud and header at the left side of the opening. Nail the others together and place them between header and sill so they coincide with the rough opening width. Toenail in, top and bottom. To open the wall, use a handsaw to cut along the lines defined by framing. If you're working from outside, use a circular saw. Refit insulation around the framing.

5 From the outside, center the unit from side to side in the rough opening. Make sure it's plumb and level (you may need to use shims), then mark the siding at the top and sides of the window.

6 Remove the window unit and cut along your marks with a circular saw (through siding only, not sheathing). Be sure to leave enough room at the top for an aluminum drip cap. Cut the drip cap to the length of the top window molding, then insert it between the siding and sheathing.

7 Lift the window into position under the drip cap. Use 10d galvanized casing nails to fasten the window to the sheathing and studs.

8 Once the unit is securely nailed in, use a good acrylic latex caulk to seal potential air leaks around the window.

9 On the inside, pack insulation into air spaces between the framing and the unit. Don't pack too tightly, or you may force the sides in too much, causing the sash to bind. Finish the interior wall with drywall, tape, and joint compound. Now attach the casing.

CHOOSING
AND INSTALLING
STORM WINDOWS

INTERIOR SASHES

Different kits are available; however, the inexpensive sheeting shown *at left* and *below, left* is probably the easiest to put in. Use scissors to trim self-adhesive molding strips and butt-join them to window casing. Cut clear sheeting to fit molding dimensions, then attach it to the strips with the tape provided. Keep sheeting taut to avoid distortion.

Another kit features snap-apart plastic molding that adheres to the window casing. Cut the acrylic plastic pane to fit and place it into the frame. Then, with a firm touch, snap the molding together for a weathertight seal around the window.

COMBINATION UNITS

Combinations fit inside your window's brick molding and sill. Set each unit into place to check for fit. Make it weathertight by running a bead of caulk at the top and sides of the frame next to the brick molding. Either skip caulking at the sill or drill small "weep" holes so rain water can escape. Set the unit into the window, and fasten with rustproof screws.

To understand the phenomenon called *heat loss*, stand in front of an undraped window on a chilly evening. It will seem to radiate cold air. Actually, heat from your home is escaping to the outside through the glass. If that same window is loose or not weather-stripped properly, cold air is also invading your house around the frame, compounding the problem.

Storm windows, outside or inside, will help prevent heat from leaving and cold air from coming in. In fact, storms can cut heat loss by as much as 50 percent. If your home has older windows without insulated glass, and your storms are antiquated and ill-fitting—if you have them at all—you're throwing money out the window.

Interior storm sashes
Interior sashes are panes of clear acrylic plastic or polypropylene sheeting set in weather-stripped molding that attaches to the window casing. They are a quick, energy-efficient, economical solution to get the benefits of double- or triple-glazing without the expense of replacing your present windows or buying exterior storms.

Available in kit form for quick installation, they're designed for custom fitting to varying window dimensions. It's also possible to fabricate your own from ⅛-inch acrylic (or flexible sheeting) and picture-frame molding.

Interior sashes do have some drawbacks, however. The most obvious is that you have to remove them to open the windows. The plastic molding provided in most kits snaps apart so you can do this without too much bother. Another disadvantage is that the acrylic or sheeting is easily scratched. It also becomes discolored when cleaned conventionally. Treat each tenderly, using only a mild liquid detergent and lots of water or a special cleaner recommended by the manufacturer.

Combination windows
Because wooden storms are rarely made today, your other option is to purchase combination screen and storm windows.

Combination windows have always been popular. They're simple to install and easy to change during the spring and fall. Plus, they're nearly maintenance-free.

Choose from combinations made of aluminum—the most widely used and reasonably priced material—or of steel, which is sturdier, longer lasting, but more expensive. Aluminum storms are available in either a natural finish, preferably anodized to retard oxidation, or baked-on colors. Steel units always feature baked-enamel finishes. Quality construction is critical; otherwise, combinations will eventually leak air and become hard to work. When you're shopping, look for windows you can operate easily, with deep tracks and lapped rather than mitered joints. Ordinarily, deeper tracks mean better insulation value.

Many suppliers offer a choice between double- and triple-track units. Triple-track designs are self-storing.

Don't forget sliding glass patio doors when installing storm windows. Two options are available. One is a ready-made storm door unit with framing and insulating glass. Installed outside like a storm window, it opens and closes. The other is a kit-form stationary sash that uses clear plastic sheeting and mounting strips and attaches to the exterior casing.

CHOOSING
WINDOW HARDWARE

New windows include the necessary operating hardware as part of the package. Generally, you choose the finish—burnished bronze, wrought iron black, brass, shiny steel, or baked-on enamel colors—for all your hinges, sash locks, and pulls.

To update an existing sash, replace the sash locks and handles on double-hungs with new ones that will look and work better. Besides choosing a finish that will blend with your decor, buy hardware that's made to last. Look for hardened steel with quality plating or baked-on color—if a piece has weight, it's probably durable. If it has movable parts, like a sash lock, check to see how smoothly it works. Be sure, too, that the hardware you select has sufficient screw holes for secure mounting.

BUYING DOORS

Doors can't stand on their looks alone. Research has shown that one exterior door lacking proper fit and weather stripping is responsible for over 6 percent of the heat loss in a home. In today's market, an energy-efficient door is also a secure one, protecting your home, your family, and the things you own. (For more on home security, see pages 114-123.)

You may want to replace an existing exterior door as part of a total face-lift—a new one does wonders for a home. You'll *definitely* want to consider replacement if it doesn't close properly, can't be effectively weather-stripped, or has cracked or broken panels or stiles. Interior doors, although they save less energy, should be replaced when they wear out or, of course, as part of a total redecorating project.

The outside story

Once you've decided upon the style of door best suited to the architectural character of your home, it's time to think about material differences. Your shopping, in fact, has only just begun.

Exterior doors are available in solid wood (plank), veneer over solid wood, veneer over a hollow core, aluminum-clad wood, steel-clad wood, and either steel or aluminum over a rigid foam core. With the exception of hollow-core exterior doors, all have insulating qualities.

Only about 1 percent of measurable heat loss occurs through the door itself, in any case. Appearance, maintenance, and security, therefore, become the critical buying points.

● *Wood doors* were used first, and their traditional appeal still makes them favorites. Wood, though a natural insulator, requires periodic painting and is subject to chipping, cracking, and shrinkage. Manufacturers of wood doors, however, have developed construction techniques that have practically eliminated these faults.

● *Aluminum and steel doors* are not solid metal, but have a lighter inner core of wood, wood and foam, or rigid foam. The aluminum or steel exterior surface comes primed or with a baked-enamel finish, is weather resistant, and doesn't swell or shrink. It's also fire retardant and, in some ways, more secure than its wood counterparts.

Air leaks around exterior doors are a major concern. To tackle the problem, complete entry "systems" have been developed. Available as pre-hung units, they include door, jamb, sill, weather stripping, and accessory components, such as sidelights. Installation takes only a few hours, and most do-it-yourselfers can handle the job. Systems come in standard rough opening sizes to accommodate remodeling projects, as well as new home construction.

Weather stripping is an important part of any exterior door. You'll get the greatest protection against drafts and water with an interlocking metal "J" strip system that forcibly

seals out cold and wet. The threshold, or sill, of a prehung exterior door should be energy efficient, too. Look for one of solid wood, preferably oak, or one with a continuous thermal break if the door is metal or metal-clad.

Hardware should be sturdy, not simply impressive, and should include a dead-bolt lock, as well as a key-locked knob-and-latch assembly for maximum security.

The inside story

Like exterior doors, their interior cousins must perform a variety of functions. They limit access, define space, and, when properly chosen, accent a decorating theme.

In years gone by, nearly all interior doors were solid wood. Today, however, hollow-core doors, primarily made of wood, are the rule; others constructed from plastic and even lightweight metal are also available. They come in a variety of types and serve a variety of purposes.

● *Panel door.* Nearly every contemporary door has a *stile,* the vertical upright on either side (and sometimes the center) of the door, and a horizontal *rail* framework. Construction like this helps to limit the wood's tendency to shrink, swell, and warp with changes in humidity. With a panel door, you can actually see the framing. Spaces between the frame members are likely to be paneled with wood, louvered slats, or glass.

● *Flush door.* The framing of a flush door is hidden beneath two or three layers of veneer. To minimize warping, each veneer runs in alternating direc-

tions, a construction technique called banding. Solid-core flush doors have dense centers of hardwood blocks or particleboard. The more common hollow-core doors use lighter materials, such as corrugated cardboard.

● *Bypass door.* This type comes in pairs. Panel or flush, solid- or hollow-core, the doors move along an overhead track, guided by metal or nylon angles screwed to the floor.

● *Folding door.* A folding door, occasionally called a bifold, has hinges holding it together. One part of the door pivots on fixed pins; the other slides along a track. For more information on bypass and folding doors, see pages 90 and 91.

See the light

Glazed patio doors, which provide easy access to the outside as well as lots of light, could be your solution for an area that needs something to perk it up. The doors currently available feature insulating glass and snug weather stripping, minimizing heat loss and air infiltration. (You'll want at least ⅝-inch tempered insulating glass, a superior seal provided by a modern weather-stripping system, and security features to limit forced entry.) Choose from the traditional bypass models or doors that swing. The doors are made of either wood, aluminum, or a combination of materials.

(continued)

BUYING DOORS
(continued)

Pocket doors are just the ticket for a narrow hall or an interior space that can't be blocked by an open door, such as in the room *above.* Here, usable work space would, at times, have been inaccessible if a standard in-swinging door had been used. Hung from an overhead track, the hollow-core door rides its rollers neatly out of sight into a "pocket" in the wall, allowing full use of the entry area.

Since pocket doors roll on self-lubricating nylon wheels, maintenance is practically nil except for occasional alignment that only requires a few turns of a screwdriver.

Consider a pocket door in new construction or a remodeling where you'll be able to add the hollow necessary to conceal it. And select a track assembly featuring a "key" opening into which the rollers enter the track. This arrangement prevents jumping.

Folding doors, as shown opening to the entertainment center *above,* are a handsome, practical solution to interior areas where there's lots of space to be covered. Closets in the hall, kitchen, bathroom, or bedroom can be attractively hidden by these bifold doors. There are also kits available that convert bifolds to multifolds, allowing four doors to fold to one side of the jamb.

These narrow doors are offered in paneled designs, and half- and full-louvered styles to enhance any interior theme. Made of wood, plastic, and, less commonly, metal, they use an overhead track, hinge, and pivot system to open and close. Adjustments are simple, and today's roller mechanisms are self-lubricating, so there's infrequent maintenance.

Bypass doors, like those *opposite,* have for many years been the answer for closets and other storage areas. Two light, hollow-core doors are

pocket

bypass

folding

suspended by movable rollers in an overhead track. Floor guides keep them in line, and allow one to bypass the other for access to the space behind. As with pocket doors, look for track assemblies that feature a key opening to prevent rollers from jumping the track. With this system, floor guides can often bend, but since they are easily repaired, this isn't a major drawback.

The miscellaneous hardware for pocket, bypass, and folding doors is shown *at right*. You'll find many finishes to choose from, but whatever look you prefer, demand durable, well-made pivots, tracks, and latches for extended service.

INSTALLING NEW DOORS

Have you always wanted easier access to the kitchen, or a door to an adjoining bedroom? Opening up an interior wall for a new doorway isn't a difficult project, even for a beginning home carpenter. In fact, it serves as a great introduction to basic framing techniques.

Special tools aren't required, but you'll have to keep everything solid, plumb, and square so the new door will work without a hitch.

Open the wall

First, decide on the location for your door, then check for any pipes, heating and cooling ducts, or electrical wires in the vicinity. You can easily reroute wires, but pipes or ducts behind the wall mean plotting another site. You'll also want to have one side of the doorway against a stud as part of the framing.

Next, use a heavy pencil to mark the dimension of your rough opening, which should be 2 inches wider and taller than the door itself. Your supplier will have the exact rough-in sizes for the unit you select.

Then, open up the wall—one side only at first—from ceiling to soleplate and to the nearest stud on either side of the new doorway. Use a hammer and chisel to break through plaster. You can cut wood lath with a saw, and metal with snips or a hacksaw, but drywall should be cut with a keyhole saw to keep dust to a minimum.

Once you've opened up the wall, you'll need to cut away a stud or two where you want the new door, then brace the opening. To do this, construct a *header* to carry the load up top and add *trimmers* to the sides. A door needs heavier framing than walls, so the door

won't sag, bind, or break from its hinges.

These instructions, as well as the step-by-step sequence *at right,* describe how to cut a doorway for a prehung unit. For a custom door, the procedures are basically the same, but the rough-in dimensions are larger.

Once you've made the opening, it's time to put the door in its place. If you're installing a prehung unit, see the box *opposite.* If you'd rather build a custom frame and hang the door yourself, see page 94.

Close the wall

If you plan to relocate a doorway, you'll have to close the old opening. In effect, the process is the reverse of that described above. Nail in some 2x4s at the top, sides, and bottom of the opening, and add a 2x4 stud in the center. Then fasten drywall in place. Tape and cover the seams, sand everything smooth, and refinish to complete the chore.

Use the right tools

To cut in a doorway and set a prehung unit, you'll need the following:
- flexible steel tape or a folding rule 12 feet long
- metal framing square
- chalk line/plumb bob
- heavy pencil
- keyhole saw
- 8- or 10-point crosscut saw, or circular saw
- 1½- and ½-inch wood chisels
- carpenter's level
- nail set
- 13- or 16-ounce claw hammer
- 10d common and 6d casing nails

(continued)

CUTTING A DOORWAY

1 One side of the new door should be next to a stud. Outline an opening 2 inches wider and taller than the size of the door. Remove the baseboard from both sides of the wall. Find studs and any electrical wires. Use a keyhole saw to cut drywall or plaster and lath inside the studs from top plate to soleplate (on one side of the wall only).

2 Cut studs near their tops and twist them free from the soleplate below. Make cuts at 87½ inches from the floor to allow for the 2x6 header you'll be installing. Leave the short pieces in place; they'll tie into the header.

3 Make the header of 2x6s, with a ½-inch spacer of plywood, to fit stud-to-stud at the top of the door. Toenail the header to the studs using the studs you removed as braces for the header. Then cut them to fit between the header and the soleplate and nail them to the studs on either side.

4 To form the rough opening width, cut two 2x4s together, and insert them between the header and soleplate at the rough opening width. Plumb, then nail in place. Use a keyhole saw to cut through the other side of the drywall. On the framing side, cut, fit, and nail drywall in place around the rough opening.

5 With a handsaw and wood chisel, remove the section of the soleplate inside the rough opening exposing the subfloor. Later, you'll need to fill the space between rooms.

PREHUNG DOORS

With the opening made, you have two choices: Cut, fit, and assemble a 12-piece frame, then hang the door; or set in a prehung unit, shim, and nail it into place.

Installing a prehung unit is more expensive than custom building, but is much less time-consuming because everything you need is already assembled.

You can order a variety of styles and sizes from lumberyards, but standard prehung units have 80x24-, 30-, and 32-inch dimensions, with a limited choice of casing moldings.

Before buying, however, measure the thickness of the wall where you want to install the door. Plaster walls require different jamb widths than drywall.

The prehung unit shown *below* is the split-jamb type, which is adjustable to varying wall thicknesses. Another kind has a removable casing on one side only.

1 Begin by removing the unit's banding and separating sections. Pull out the double-headed nail, which holds the door to the jamb on the latch side, but don't remove any of the spacer blocks. Set the frame and door into your rough opening. Plumb the door frame, then nail the casing to the wall studs with 6d casing nails.

2 Move to the other side, and install shims between jamb and stud at the point where the spacer blocks touch the door. Insert the other half of the frame into the grooved section and nail the casing to the wall. Then nail through the stop into the jambs. Open the door and remove the spacers. Check to see if the door works properly, then cut the tie straps at the bottom of the jamb sides.

FRAMING AND HANGING A DOOR

1 Consider also custom building a new doorway. Use 1-inch stock, as wide as your walls are thick, for top and side jambs. You can buy stops and trim pieces from stock at a lumberyard. Cut the head (top) jamb to the width of the door, plus ⅝ inch. Side jambs should equal the distance between the bottom of the header and the floor. Join head and side jambs as shown, and set the frame.

2 Level the head jamb, and plumb the sides, using pieces of wood shingle as shims. Insert the shims at head, hinge, and latch levels, and near the bottom. Use a long, straight board with a level to help straighten and plumb the side jambs. Once everything is square and plumb, nail the jamb into the studs and header with 8d casing nails. (You'll have to go through the shims.)

3 Measure the door's width and height, checking the width at several points. The door should clear the jambs by ⅛ inch at the top and sides, ⅜ inch at the bottom (more over a carpet). Never remove more than ¾ inch from the top or bottom of a hollow-core door. For easier closing, use a jack or jointer plane to bevel the knob side of the new door approximately 3½ degrees.

4 The size and number of hinges will vary, depending on the type and thickness of the door. Hollow-core doors, for example, don't require as heavy a hinge as solid ones. (This 1⅜-inch door has three 3½x3½-inch butt hinges.) The top hinge should be 7 inches from the top of the door; the lowest hinge, 11 inches from the bottom. Center the third hinge. Use a 1¼-inch wood chisel to mortise hinges level with the edge's surface.

5 Tack the door stop temporarily into the jamb. Set the door into the jamb, shimming up from the bottom and sides until it fits squarely into the opening. Mark the top and bottom of all three hinges on the edge of the door jamb. Remove the door and mortise for hinges. Pull hinge pins, attach their leaves to the door and jamb, and fit the door into the jamb. Mate the hinge leaves, insert pins, and the door should swing freely.

CHOOSING HINGES

There are many kinds of hinges—decorative and invisible, one-directional or two, self-closing or standard.

Most interior doors have common butt hinges, which are either right- or left-handed. A right-handed hinge is on your right when the door opens away from you, *vice versa* for the left-handed type. In either case, don't try using a hinge turned upside down—the pin will fall out.

The proper size and weight of a hinge are determined by the thickness and weight of the door. An average hollow-core interior door, for example, should have 3½-inch, medium-weight hinges.

Finishes vary, too. Brass or bronze plate, stainless or wrought iron are the most common. Depending upon size and finish, prices range from $3 to $15 a pair.

INSTALLING A KNOB SET

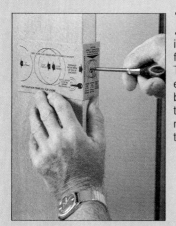

1 Using an awl and the template included with the instructions, mark positions for the knob-assembly holes. The knob should be 37 inches from the floor. Its hole will be 2⅜ or 2¾ inches from the edge of the door. To measure accurately, fold the template as indicated.

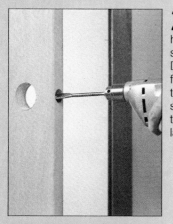

2 With an expansive bit on your electric drill, bore a hole into the door to the size specified for the lock tube. Drill first from one side, then from the other to avoid splintering the wood. Use a spade bit to drill a hole into the edge of the door for the latch and assembly.

3 Follow the instructions provided to insert the cylinder assembly and latch into the door. Fit the interior knob on the barrel of the lock tube and secure. Check to make sure the knob-and-latch assemblies work properly.

4 Place the strike plate over the door latch, and mark the position of the door edge on the plate's top and bottom. This will help you later when you're aligning the plate on the door jamb. Remove the plate and close the door. With a sharp pencil, pinpoint the spot where the center of the latch hits the door jamb.

5 Hold the strike plate to the door jamb, centering the hole over the pencil mark you made for the latch. Also, make sure it's flush with the top and bottom marks indicating the edge of the door. On the door jamb, trace the location of the strike plate and the latch keeper.

6 With a sharp wood chisel, cut a mortise into the jamb equal to the depth of the strike plate. If you cut too deep, use cardboard to raise the plate so it's flush. To make room for the latch, use a drill or chisel to bore a hole into the center of the strike plate. Fasten the strike plate to the jamb with screws, after checking the alignment one more time.

DOOR HARDWARE

Door hardware falls into two categories—necessary and ornamental. Hinges, knob-and-latch assemblies, and locks are necessary. Escutcheon plates, knockers, and mail slots, though functional, are highly decorative additions.

For either, select quality, name-brand door hardware that will give years of dependable service. Look for heavy-gauge metal, fine machining without sharp, rough edges or knurls, and a plated finish to withstand heavy use.

Match the hardware to the door. Not only must it blend with the style or type of door you've chosen, it must also do its job properly. A solid slab entry door, for instance, must be hung with heavy-duty hinges.

Think about security, too. A lockset with key, combined with a dead-bolt assembly, gives greater peace of mind.

Door hardware is available in numerous styles, from sleek contemporary to detailed Spanish designs, and in various materials, from burnished aluminum to solid brass. But when shopping, buy with durability and craftsmanship in mind first. Once you've found a manufacturer's hardware that meets your criteria, select the style that complements your home.

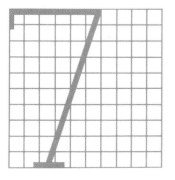

SAVE ENERGY

How you treat your windows and doors affects not just the way they look, but also your comfort and utility bills. The right treatments help seal in heat on cold days and deflect it on hot ones. This chapter explores the ins and outs of heat losses and gains by presenting an array of interior and exterior products designed specifically to conserve energy. You'll also learn about the ways traditional treatments can accomplish the same thing. But first, let's survey your windows and doors from an energy point of view.

HOW DO YOUR WINDOWS AND DOORS RATE?

Any survey of the ways your windows and doors conserve energy depends upon some factors you can control and some you just have to make the best of. One you can't do much about is the orientation of your windows and doors. Start your survey by noting which directions they face.

The large drawing *opposite* shows the ideal energy-wise home—large openings for light and solar heat gain facing primarily south, small- to medium-size windows on the east and west, and no openings (or very small ones) on the north side. If you're planning a new home or addition, position windows and doors for greatest energy efficiency. If your present home is less than ideal, make it more efficient by taking into account its orientation.

In winter, when the sun travels in a lower arc in the sky, let its free heat warm your home by uncovering east-facing windows in the morning. At night, seal all windows to help retain warmth. If someone is at home during the day, you'll benefit further by uncovering south-facing windows during the day, and west-facing windows in late afternoon.

In summer, when the sun moves in a higher arc and keeping cool is your concern, block as much heat transmission as possible by keeping windows (especially those facing south and west) covered during the daytime. At night, uncover them to let in cool evening breezes.

On the north side of the house, where solar heat gain is virtually nonexistent, open windows in summer to admit cool morning and evening air.

Seal up all energy leaks

Your next line of defense against rising utility costs is to make sure that your doors and windows are in good condition and are weathertight. Do you have any broken or cracked windows that are allowing heat to escape all winter long? How about windows that have not been caulked—or those with caulk that has become ineffective because it is old and cracked? Are your windows made of double- or triple-pane glass, or do you have tight-fitting storm windows? Are your exterior doors insulated, and have you installed good weather stripping?

When you're surveying your doors, don't forget to take a look at any attic openings you may have. Make sure there is adequate insulation above the attic door, and that the door itself fits tightly so heated air doesn't rise up and out of the house. If the door fits loosely, consider sealing the edges with duct tape or strips of foam weather stripping.

Once your windows and doors are as weathertight as you can make them, consider investing in energy-saving window treatments. You can expect a single pane of uncovered glass to lose between five and ten times more heat than the surrounding insulated walls. Even double- and triple-glazed windows can still funnel a surprising amount of heat out of your home in winter, and act as solar collectors in summer, admitting unwanted heat. The following pages show window treatments and other measures that can help you control these losses and gains.

south

west

east

north

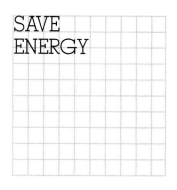
WITH CURTAINS AND DRAPERIES

Although they are among the most popular window treatments, traditional curtains and draperies don't do much to prevent heat from rushing out through your windows. A few remedial steps can let you keep the softness and charm of pleated or shirred curtains and draperies without sacrificing energy efficiency. Here are ways to back up your curtains and draperies with thermal and heat-reflective liners, create heat-saving seals for the sides, tops, and bottoms of your windows, and save energy by layering other products behind your existing window treatments.

The shiny drapery liner shown *opposite* is one product that will help you improve the efficiency of traditional draperies. It and similar thermal liners are available through drapery shops and some large catalog stores. This liner installs in minutes; just hang it behind your present draperies or curtains on the existing hooks.

During the winter, face the shiny side toward the room to radiate household heat back inside; in summer, face the shiny side outward to fend off sunlight and exterior heat.

Also, look for draperies made of medium-weight fabrics and tight weaves. Better yet, aim for layers of fabrics or choose materials with an acrylic foam backing. If you are ordering custom-made window treatments, ask if insulating or reflective linings are available.

Seal up

The best of materials will only go so far in conserving energy. Unless you have a snug seal between the curtain or drapery and the window frame, air moving from a warm room toward a cold window can set up a convection current that speeds the movement of heated air out of your home.

To avoid heat losses around the top and sides, add a cornice above the draperies, or surround them with a *lambrequin*, which looks like a cornice with sides reaching to the floor. Hanging draperies from the ceiling and allowing them to touch the sill or floor is another solution. To seal draperies to the walls at the sides, sew Velcro® or magnetic tape to draperies, and tack the same material to corresponding places on the wall. Finish by sealing fabric to fabric where panels meet in the center of the window.

THE LAYERED LOOK

Layering heat-retaining treatments behind your existing window blinds, curtains, or draperies is one way to add efficiency without sacrificing your favorite window treatments. You can layer a shade behind virtually any covering you now enjoy on your windows.

Adding a properly installed roller shade is one of the easiest and most economical ways to save home heating dollars. A shade can cut winter heat loss through windows by 30 to 35 percent.

For maximum insulating value, buy shades made of impermeable material, such as vinyl-coated cloth, and mount them inside the window casings. This seals air between the shade and the window, forming a barrier against heat and cold. When down, the shade should be close to—but not touching—the window glass. The shade's sides should be no more than ¼ inch from the sides of the window.

Sealing the top, sides, and bottom of even an ordinary window shade will dramatically improve its energy-saving properties. To seal the top, fasten a V-shaped strip of flexible plastic or rubber to the top of the window casing with screws. The strip should rest atop the shade without hampering its movement.

To seal the bottom edge against the windowsill, first add drapery weights to the shade's bottom dowel. Then secure self-adhesive foam weather stripping along the sill. When the shade is down, it should rest on the weather stripping.

A simple roller shade not only will cut drafts and save winter heat, it also helps your windows deflect summertime heat. For maximum heat and light deflection, look for reflective shade fabric, and be sure to mount the shade with the reflective side facing outdoors.

Another option is to sew a "window mat" that you press tightly to the window casing at night behind your existing draperies or other window treatments. The mat is an easy-to-make flat "sandwich" of materials— quilted batting, plastic sheeting that acts as a vapor barrier, and your own decorative fabric. Stitch the layers of material together, sewing lengths of magnetic tape into the edges on all four sides. Apply magnetic tape to your window casing. At night, simply press the mat into place. During the day, roll the mat up as a bolster for your sofa or bed.

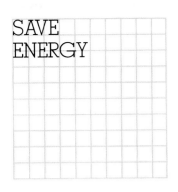

SAVE ENERGY

WITH THERMAL SHADES

Thick thermal shades blanket your windows with a cozy layer of insulation between you and the outdoors. You can buy quilted or layered thermal shades in many department and catalog store drapery departments, as well as window specialty shops. Too, you can make your own or have them custom-made with an inner layer of batting added for insulation. But first, let's look at the key criteria for any insulated window covering, then discuss a couple of examples.

Before you buy or make thermal shades, it's important to understand what makes any window treatment energy-saving.

First, look for treatments with an inner core of insulation. (In shades, that might be a layer of quilted batting. In shutters and rigid panels, it might consist of rigid insulation board.)

Second, the thermal window covering should have a layer of vapor barrier (such as plastic sheeting) to minimize damaging condensation between the treatment and the window glass itself. Third, the covering should have a reflective surface (such as aluminum foil or light-colored fabric) facing outside to deflect summer sun. Finally, select a complementary decorative facing material.

The shades shown on these pages are good examples of products that meet these guidelines. In the potentially chilly north-facing bedroom *below*, what looks like an ordinary Roman shade is actually a highly effective insulator. It's a do-it-yourself project that starts with a quilted sandwich of insulation and vapor barrier available by the yard in many fabric stores. (You choose your own decorative fabric to cover the insulated lining.) When lowered at night, the shade seals snugly to the window casing with magnetic tape, providing an R-factor of about 7.5 when used over fixed single glazing.

For large windows, a variation on the first shade idea is shown *opposite*. It runs on a track and folds up into pleats like a Roman shade. It can span large widths and heights—even on curved greenhouse glass. Here, the shade is covered in the same bright floral print used for the tablecloth and chair pads.

WITH PANELS
AND SHUTTERS

The three essentials for energy-saving window treatments—a core of insulation, a vapor barrier, and a reflective facing—are packaged in many different forms. If thermal shades aren't your style, rigid pop-in panels may be the solution. They are easy to make, easy on your budget, and can be designed to complement almost any decor. Or add old-fashioned charm along with insulation in the form of updated shutters.

At night, pop-in panels *at upper right* fit tightly within the window casing to seal the glass against drafts and heat loss. During the day, the panels become a decorative folding screen for a reading corner, *opposite*.

To make the panels, wrap rigid insulation board with polyethylene (for a vapor barrier) and decorative fabric. For a softer look, glue or staple a layer of batting to the interior side of the panels before covering them with fabric. Small fabric tabs provide pulls to easily remove the panels. To construct the "screen," make grooved wooden bases and cover them with fabric. Slide the panels into the bases and position as needed.

Shutters

If shutters are more to your liking, make or buy insulated versions like the ones shown *at lower right.* Mount them inside your window casing or, as shown here, order them prehinged to moldings that replace your existing window trim. The panels are 1⅜ inches thick, with birch plywood over a hardwood frame. A ¾-inch core of insulation (faced with reflective foil) and a lining of flexible foam weather stripping along all the edges help the shutters achieve an estimated R-factor of 9.1.

For a similar shuttered look at a do-it-yourself price, consider making your own insulated shutters. Use 1-inch-thick rigid foam wrapped with foil and then with a decorative covering (fabric, wallpaper, even thin wooden strips). Frame the foam board with 1x2s. Measure carefully and hinge so shutters fit snugly within your window casing. Add weather stripping so edges seal tightly when the shutters are closed.

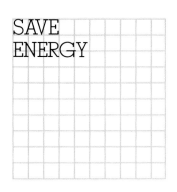
WITH INTERIOR SHADING SYSTEMS

Take a minute to stand before an unshaded sunny window, and you'll experience first-hand the naturally warm "greenhouse effect" pouring in through even a small area of glass. Free solar heat that's so welcome in winter becomes a costly and unpleasant guest in summer. If you rely on air conditioning or electric fans to cool your home in summer, you'll reduce your energy load by using one or a combination of shading systems to keep unwanted heat out of the house.

Although the most efficient form of window shading consists of an awning or other device placed outside your home (see pages 108-111), you can still reap comfortable, money-saving benefits by installing reflective window treatments inside.

The photo *opposite* shows a sampling of some specially designed products for interior shading.

Adhesive film
One good energy-saver is a reflective film *opposite, bottom right* that adheres to window glass. The film's reflective surface redirects sunlight to the outside.

The usual window film is a tinted polyester sheet with a thin coating of aluminum. It is this aluminum layer that gives the film its reflective quality. Viewing the outdoors through a film-covered window is similar to looking through sunglasses. Most films offer an additional bonus—privacy. You can see out, but from the outside, passersby see only a mirrorlike surface.

Not only can films keep you cooler, but they'll also reduce the fading, discoloration, and deterioration of household carpeting, rugs, upholstery fabrics, and of other materials that excessive sunlight can cause.

Films vary in the amount of shading they provide. A tinted plastic film without a metallized layer reflects about 25 percent of the sun's heat; aluminized films reflect as much as 80 percent of the heat and light. The film *opposite* comes in silver, bronze, or smoke shades

and is reusable season after season. To install, peel off the clear protective layer as shown in the *top inset photo, opposite.* Adhere the film to the window with water and press into place as shown in *center inset photo, opposite.* Smooth out any air bubbles with a squeegee. Films provide good sun control in the summer, but they generally must be removed in winter to allow windows to admit the welcomed solar heat.

Roller film
The roller film blind shown on the window *opposite* can be installed in a track and left there year-round. In winter, roll it up during the day to let in sunlight; at night, pull down the film to seal off the window and reduce heat loss. Unlike adhesive film applied directly to the window, the roller blind creates a dead-air space between the film and the glass. This helps insulate your home in winter. The film also reflects heated air back into your room for more energy savings.

Mini-slat blinds
Horizontal or vertical blinds offer another way to fend off heat and light without totally cutting off your view of the outside world. The mini-slat blind *opposite* helps deflect much of the sunlight that strikes it. Made of 1-inch steel louvers that can be adjusted as needed, the blind has a rust-resistant enamel finish. Some mini-slat blinds have a reflective metallic coating on one side of the slats and a dark heat-absorbing color on the other. In summer, face the metallic side out to deflect sun and heat; in winter, face the dark side out to absorb them.

Usually, the angle of the slats is controlled manually by a cord or rod tilt mechanism, but motorized—even solar-powered—models are also available. The latter model tilts its slats automatically as the sun hits them. Solar heat drives a piston-type rod which in turn activates a tilt-drive shaft. The slats return to the open position when the sun is obscured. This type of mechanism is ideal for hard-to-reach locations such as skylights and clerestories.

Making the most of traditional treatments
Specialty products like the ones shown are designed with energy efficiency in mind, but ordinary shades, curtains, or draperies also help deflect unwelcome sun and heat as long as they are light-colored on the outside. Traditional treatments reflect some—but not all—incoming heat back out through the windows.

Although interior shading devices are a great improvement over uncovered glass, they still allow heat to build up in the space between the window and the blind or curtain. If air conditioning is not being used, be sure to open the window (at top and bottom, if possible) to vent this hot air. Not only will venting make your home more comfortable, it also will minimize the damage to window trim and window treatments that excessive heat can sometimes cause.

SAVE ENERGY

Interior shading can reduce the amount of sunlight that penetrates directly into a room and heats up the air inside. But when sun hits a window, the glass itself also heats up and much of this heat can radiate indoors. This is why the very best way to shade windows is from the outside—keep the sun from hitting the glass in the first place, and you drastically reduce heat radiation. Here's a sampling of products which do just that.

WITH EXTERIOR SHADING SYSTEMS

The photo *at left* gives you an idea of the variety of exterior shading devices you can buy for your home.

One solution: Roll-up exterior shutters are a recent import from Europe, where they have been used for nearly a century. The adjustable design *at upper far left* and *upper near left* (inset) offers total shading, shading with ventilation, or a completely unobstructed view. Along its edges, each slat interlocks with the next using expandable tongue-and-groove connections. The shutter runs up and down in tracks to keep it tight against the window.

As the shutter is raised, its expandable connections stretch. This stretching opens spaces between the slats, admitting filtered natural light and fresh air. When desired, the shutter can be pulled up all the way and stored in a roll enclosure on the outside of the house above the window.

You can operate roll-up exterior shutters from inside the house with either manual or electric controls. The shutters also protect windows from storms, high winds, debris, break-ins, and vandalism. They even have a small—but positive—effect on winter heat loss. The shutters shown here are available in widths up to 20 feet. They come with either wooden or plastic slats, and with either an electric or manual pulley system.

Solar screens

Woven sun screens are a good bet if you're seeking an easy-to-install product. These mesh screens offer low-cost shading, ventilation, and protection from insects.

Although much like conventional wire screens, sun screens differ in that they are made from thicker materials especially woven to block sunlight.

Sun screens not only stop the sun's heat before it enters your home, they also provide added privacy, yet the view from inside is only slightly obscured.

The solar screen *at lower far left* is a fiber-glass mesh with white or silver aluminum edge framing and special corner locks. It comes in do-it-yourself kits in widths to 48 inches. A companion kit for combination windows also is available. Solar screens of either fiber-glass or aluminum mesh also come in rolls up to 84 inches wide.

Mini-louvers

An alternative to screens is a mini-louver system. Mini-louvers borrow an old shading concept—the traditional louvered exterior shutter—and update it with modern manufacturing techniques. The most important change is the reduced size of the louvers—a slim $\frac{1}{16}$ inch wide.

Each mini-louver slat is held at a fixed angle to shade the window from overhead sun. While blocking direct sunlight, mini-louvers still provide a surprisingly good view from indoors. They also increase privacy and allow simultaneous shade and ventilation.

Install mini-louvers mounted in conventional or specially designed screen frames outside the window; remove them in the winter if you prefer.

The example shown *at lower near left* works on conventional—or even slanting—windows to minimize heat gain and glare.

SAVE ENERGY

Awnings are making a comeback, thanks to a new generation of energy-conscious consumers. Homeowners are rediscovering how efficiently awnings reduce heat gain through windows. In fact, awnings can cut your air conditioning bill by as much as 25 percent. Today's awnings offer updated styling, greater versatility, colorful and durable fabrics, and even automatic controls.

WITH AWNINGS

Today's fabric awnings are made of newly developed materials that are sturdy and will keep their good looks through many summers. The fabric awning shown *opposite* is made of acrylic cloth, but you can choose from acrylic-painted army duck, vinyl-coated duck, and vinyl-laminated polyester as well.

Other recent advances by fabric awning makers are the mechanisms that are used to retract and extend the fabric. Some of these retractors operate manually; others are motorized. Some motorized controls have automatic switches that go into action at dawn and dusk, and moisture-sensitive controls that retract the fabric whenever it rains.

Styling
The simplest style is a "hood" awning made of a metal frame covered with fabric. The enclosed sides block sunlight from left and right as well as from straight ahead. A hinge attaches the horizontal frame to the house so the awning can be folded up against the side of the house during harsh weather.

Adjustable, retractable fabric awnings with open sides have one disadvantage—they don't block sunlight that hits the window from the left or right.

Aluminum alternatives
Aluminum shading devices will last for years, and they are strong enough to remain on the house all year long. When properly installed, they can withstand high winds, rain, hail, and even the weight of snow. Many aluminum awnings are fixed, but you can find adjustable models. The photos *at right* show a sampling of some readily available aluminum awnings.

The awning *at top right* and *below* rolls down to keep out the sun and rolls back up when it's not needed. It sports a durable baked-on enamel finish and comes in widths from 30 inches to 144 inches. The awning is 48 inches deep and fits windows from 40 to 70 inches high.

Also shown *at center right* is a mansard design that offers

the added energy bonus of enclosed sides for maximum sun reflection. This awning is available in widths from 31½ to 63 inches, with a 29-inch drop and a 24-inch projection out from the window.

A less solid barrier is the open-slat awning shown *at bottom right*. The open-slat styling permits a partial view, but it also allows more sunlight inside. The awning has adjustable support arms that control its angle. This 10-slat model works for windows up to 42 inches high, in widths from 36 to 60 inches.

Shop around
When you're shopping for awnings, check large catalog stores as well as local awning companies. Local dealers usually will give you a free estimate for their awnings and installation. Catalogs offer flexible sizing and install-it-yourself products.

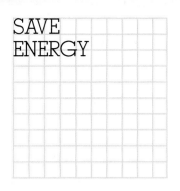
WITH AN
AIR-LOCK ENTRY

Each time you enter or leave your home, a few of your costly energy dollars sneak out. One way to plug the leak is by creating an air-lock entry. The term "air lock" may sound a bit formidable, but it simply means a well-sealed intermediate space between the outside and the inside of your house. Pioneers often added a lean-to at the back door to conserve heat and keep winter winds out of the main house. A modern-day enclosed back porch performs a similar function. Or add an air-lock vestibule to any doorway: Along with energy savings, you'll also gain some valuable living space.

While you can't avoid opening your doors, you can minimize the flow of cold winter air (or warm air in the summer) into your home by adding an air-lock vestibule. The first step is to understand how one works.

A true air lock traps air pressure between an inner and an outer door. If you close one before you open the other, the indoor and outdoor air pressures can't interact. That means no strong drafts. This is an obvious temperature control asset in winter, but it will also keep your home cooler in the summer.

To do the most good, add an air-lock vestibule where doors create unpleasant drafts by opening directly into often-used living areas or interior traffic lanes. This is likely to be on the north or northwest side of your home, where winter winds are strongest.

The home shown *opposite* is a good example of an air-lock entry at work. The back door of this two-story Victorian house in New Hampshire opened directly into a drafty service hall. Every time someone opened the back door, a chilly blast of air blew into the kitchen, the dining room, and the basement stairway. To make things more comfortable, the owners added a well-proportioned glassed-in air lock. Their new rear entry has become a pavilionlike vestibule, complete with a slate floor sealed with clear acrylic to protect it from muddy boots and dripping umbrellas.

In addition to the energy savings and increased comfort

inside the home, the air lock has added bonus space, which relieves traffic problems in the once-cramped rear hallway.

Close in a porch
If your home already has a small entry porch, you're halfway there. All you may need to do is enclose the sides of your existing stoop and add a storm door—a project you may be able to complete in a couple of weekends.

In the photo *above*, the entry porch was enclosed with small-pane fixed-glass panels. For summertime ventilation, the glass panel in the outer door is replaced with a screen. The styling complements this older home so well that passersby can't tell if the enclosed entry is new or an original feature of the house. Although this air lock measures only 40 by 60

inches inside, there's plenty of room to close the outer door before opening the inner one.

If you're considering an air-lock entry, design your structure to complement your home's architecture. Plan window styles, fascia boards, and the siding of the entry to match the rest of the house.

Or build in
If you don't want to alter the look of your home's exterior, consider creating a vestibule *inside*. Again, all you need is enough floor space to close one door before opening the other. You might want to add or expand storage near the entry at the same time. Interior air locks are less expensive than exterior versions, because you needn't invest in roofing and foundation materials.

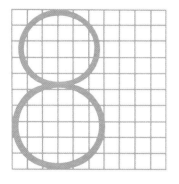

SECURING YOUR HOME

As any law officer will tell you, now is the best time to beef up your home's security. Wait until after an intruder strikes—as too many people do—and you've waited too long. Obviously, secure windows and doors are a front-line defense, and bolstering yours is an effective way to discourage would-be burglars. This chapter shows how lights, locks, and alarms—along with a more security-minded attitude on your part—can go a long way toward safeguarding your house and easing your mind.

Being on the safe side is, to a large degree, a way of living. The best first step you can take against intruders is to adopt a daily routine that makes your house and family less vulnerable to crime. For example, make a point of locking the door behind you, even if you're just visiting a neighbor. And always take the key along; don't leave it in the mailbox or under a doormat—places where most burglars look. In fact, whether you're staying home or not, it's a good idea to lock all accessible windows and doors when you're not using them.

Keep in mind, too, that potential intruders are often good actors. When a stranger comes to the door dressed in a repairman's uniform or trimly attired in well-tailored clothing, don't automatically assume he's there on legitimate business. Before allowing him in, ask to see his credentials, checking them through a wide-angle peephole or nearby window. (If you have one, speak through an intercom.) If you have doubts, note the organization he represents and, while he waits outside, call to confirm his association.

Vacation ideas

If you're leaving for more than a day, ask the local police and trustworthy neighbors to keep an eye on the house while you're gone, and take these other steps to give your home a "lived-in" look.

• Stop mail and newspaper deliveries so material doesn't collect in your mailbox or on your doorstep.
• Use timers that periodically turn on lights, television, and radio during evening hours when you're normally awake.
• Keep curtains and shades partly open.

• Park a car in the driveway.
• Have a friend or relative cut the grass or shovel snow while you're away.
• Ask a neighbor to use one or more of your trash cans and carry them out to the street on collection day.

Safe-keeping

Always stash highly portable valuables such as cash, negotiable securities, or jewelry in a well-hidden safe, or store them at your bank. Another good item for a safety deposit box is a complete inventory of every valuable in the house, including physical descriptions, purchase slips, model numbers, brand names, and photos of smaller items.

To collect insurance—should a burglar strike—you may need an inventory to prove your losses. And make sure you *can* collect. Check the personal property coverage of your homeowners policy to see if it adequately covers every valuable you own. If it doesn't, update the policy.

It also may pay to participate in Operation Identification. Sponsored by local law enforcement agencies, this program—which involves etching an I.D. number on valuables with a special electric pen—has caused many a burglar to think twice, and then forget the whole thing.

The house illustrated at right features three broad categories of protective strategies. Most crime specialists believe that if you can stall an intruder's entry with locks, expose his suspicious activities with effective lighting and landscaping, or call attention to his presence with a loud alarm, you'll probably send him away empty-handed.

ANATOMY OF A WELL-SECURED HOUSE

1 Burglar bars on basement windows
2 Timers on lights, TV, and radio
3 Keyed sash lock
4 Magnetic sensors on doors and windows wired to alarm control panel
5 Impact-resistant acrylic in place of glass

6 Pressure mat wired to alarm control panel
7 Photoelectric eye wired to alarm control panel
8 Alarm control panel
9 Floodlights along walls that have windows and doors
10 Alarm siren to alert neighbors and scare off intruder

11 Garage door closed, except when in use
12 Shrubs trimmed back around doors and windows
13 Post lamp
14 Two main entrance lights (For other entrances, one light located on the lock side of the door is sufficient.)
15 Intercom for talking to strangers

16 Wide-angle peephole
17 Dead-bolt locks backed up for reinforcement
18 Solid-core door
19 Operation Indentification and alarm system window stickers

PROTECTING
WINDOWS

Window shopping is a favorite pastime for many burglars. That's because inadequately protected windows are easy marks for intruders who know how to force them without too much effort, and then climb in unnoticed.

Fortunately, reinforcing the windows in your home is neither difficult nor expensive. Most measures require—should you do the work yourself—just a little skill, a few basic tools, and hardware like the items *opposite*.

Window watch

First survey the windows at your house. Check out each for its ability to withstand an intruder's attack, paying special attention to basement windows and any that can be reached from ground level. Then list each on paper, noting its type and the locking mechanism currently securing it.

As you work, keep in mind that on most windows you'll need to replace the original locks with sturdy, reliable ones. Ordinary sash locks on double-hung windows squeeze out drafts but provide little security. An intruder can simply insert a knife between the sashes and turn the lock to its open position, or exert enough pressure to snap the hardware. A key-operated lock is a good replacement; even if a burglar breaks or cuts a small hole in the glass, he won't be able to reach in and open the lock.

Windows don't always have to be closed to shut out potential thieves. Some locks allow you to secure a window and still leave it partly open for ventilation. No matter how your windows are protected, whether they're locked or secured in some other way, think about how you and your family could exit through them in case of an emergency. Keep keys nearby and make sure everyone knows where they are.

Why all the fuss about window locks when an intruder can simply break glass to get in? The reason is that shattering glass attracts attention, and most burglars don't like audiences. If you don't feel secure about glass, replace it with impact-resistant acrylic or polycarbonate. Another (although less attractive) alternative is to install a metal grille outside the window or a scissors-type gate inside. Some gates have quick-release levers for emergency exiting. Keep in mind that a stationary grille renders its window useless as a fire exit.

Up-to-date protection

Once you know which windows to strengthen, you have to know how to go about doing it. The next step is to develop a list of all the hardware you'll need. For help in finding out what's available, look over the drawings on this page and on page 118. They'll give you a good idea of the best ways to protect different kinds of windows; they also explain how to install these protective devices and other simple reinforcements.

If you don't want to do the work yourself, another option, of course, is to hire a locksmith or carpenter to do it for you. Professional services will, in all likelihood, yield professional-looking results—but at about twice the price of doing the job on your own.

(continued)

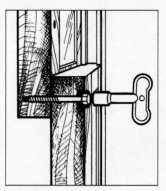

1 One way to secure double-hung windows is to install an inexpensive lag-screw system. To do it, insert the screws through recessed, cuplike washers and into joining sash rails. Then tighten, using a special key provided with the hardware. Another hole or two lower on the bottom sash lets you lock the window in partially open positions for ventilation.

2 Or here's an even easier way to protect double-hung windows. With this method, you won't have to purchase any special hardware. Cut a piece of scrap wood you can wedge between the top of the frame and the parting strip atop the lower sash. Of course, this strategy doesn't look as tidy, and you can't secure the window when it's open.

3 A bolt-action, keyed lock also strengthens double-hung windows. Install it on the top rail of the bottom sash, flush to one side of the upper sash. Keep the key near enough for quick emergency exit, but out of reach of a burglar's exploring hand. To secure windows in an open position and provide ventilation, drill extra holes into the upper sash.

4 One final protective measure for this kind of window features a keyed lock with a lever. Position it on the top and center of the parting rails. The lock illustrated here features an indicator button on the right side of the housing that lets you know whether the window is secured. When the button is out, the window is unlocked; when it's in, the window is locked.

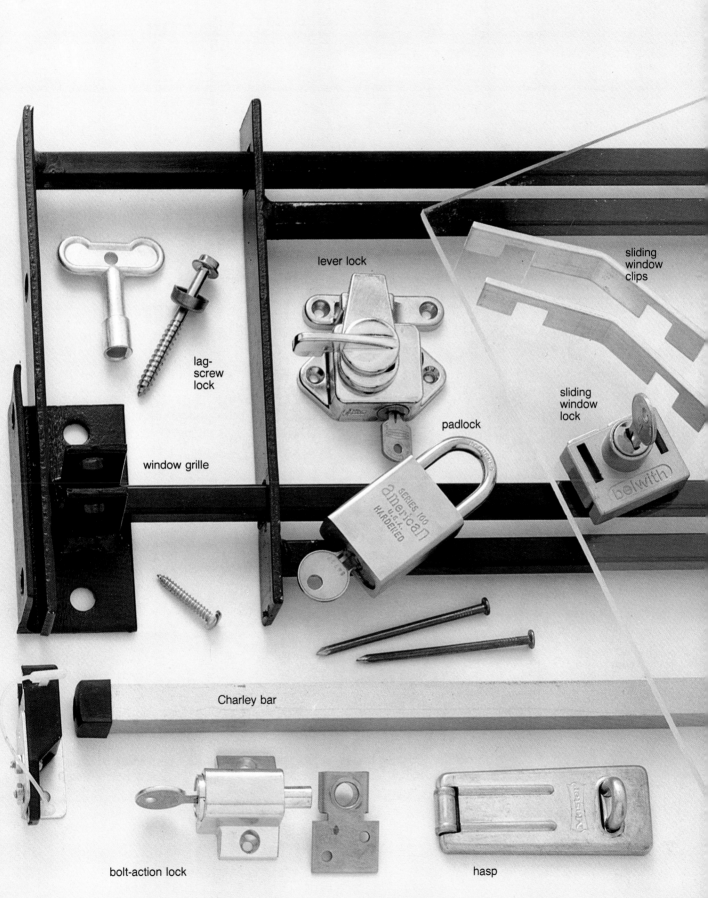

lever lock

sliding
window
clips

lag-
screw
lock

sliding
window
lock

padlock

window grille

Charley bar

bolt-action lock

hasp

117

PROTECTING WINDOWS

(continued)

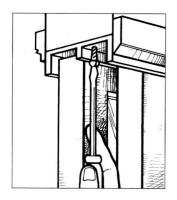

1 You can secure a casement window in just a few seconds: Simply remove the crank from the operator (but place it nearby in case of emergencies). If you prefer a lock and key, choose a lock similar to this one. Use screws to install it along the sash rail. Another alternative is to install the same type of chain lock used on doors. Attach with the biggest screws possible.

2 What homeowners don't know about their sliding windows can hurt them. Most lift up and out of their tracks with the greatest of ease. Prevent intruders from entering this way by inserting sheet metal screws into the upper track. Adjust the screws so the window just clears them, leaving no room to maneuver the window out of its track.

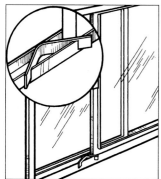

3 All savvy burglars have an easy time prying open poorly protected sliding windows. With only a little pressure, they can snap the brittle metal catch holding the window closed. Stop them in their tracks by inserting a metal clip into the lower track and against the closed window. The clip can be bent by hand to adjust to channel thickness.

4 Sturdy lock-and-key sets are another way to secure sliding windows. To install one, drill holes for the screws and bolt at the location shown, then fasten the lock in place. Note how the mechanism works when in the lock position. To secure windows in an open position, drill additional holes. This type of lock also works on vertical sliding aluminum windows.

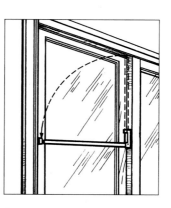

5 A Charley bar should also provide all the holding power needed to stop a burglar from prying open a sliding glass window. Easy to install with just a few screws, the bar can be raised when it's not being used and held by a clip in the "up" position. The bar keeps the windows from sliding, but doesn't preclude jimmying the unit up and out of the track.

6 Because they're often shielded by window wells or shrubbery, basement windows have long been easy marks for experienced crooks. Thwart their attempts by installing a sturdy hasp and keyed padlock. Keep the key nearby so you can easily open the window for ventilation or in case it's needed for emergency exiting.

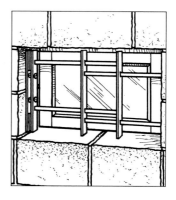

7 An even better way of closing off a basement window is to screw burglar bars or a piece of ¼-inch strap metal across the opening with one-way screws and wall anchors. In a high-crime neighborhood, consider using glass blocks to wall up the opening completely. These methods rule out using the window for an emergency exit.

8 Occasionally, a burglar will break the glass pane of a window (or door) to reach an inside lock. You can prevent this by replacing the glass in your most vulnerable windows and doors with impact-resistant acrylic or polycarbonate. For detailed instructions about reglazing both wood- and metal-framed windows, see pages 144-146.

PROTECTING DOORS

Like windows, haphazardly protected doors are easy pickings for most burglars. Again, carefully inspect yours from an intruder's point of view.

First, tap on every hinged exterior door to hear how it's made. If a door sounds hollow, one swift kick could do it in. Replace with a 1¾-inch, solid-core door that fits tightly inside a strong frame made of wood or metal.

Apply pressure to the jambs near each door lock. Do they bow outward? If so, placing shims behind them will stop a thief from using his screwdriver or pry bar to pop bolts and latches free of their strike plates.

If any hinged exterior doors swing outward, the barrels on their hinges are probably on the outside. An enterprising intruder could pull the pins from the barrels and lift the door completely out of its frame. To block that possibility, install metal pins and sleeves on the interior surface of the door and jamb, as shown on page 121.

Locking up

A good lock, of course, is essential to any door's security. If you're relying on a conventional key-in-knob version, beware: It offers little deterrent to thieves. Many key-in-knob locks can be easily jimmied by sliding a credit card between the door edge and strike plate, and breaking off the knob renders this type useless.

Make your primary lock a dead bolt with a 1-inch bolt throw. Typical residential locksets are designed to be mortised into the door, like the ones shown *above* and *bot-*

tom, right. The version *above* also includes a jimmy-resistant strike that can't be slipped with a credit card.

If an intruder could reach the lock by breaking a nearby window, consider purchasing a double-cylinder dead bolt, like the one pictured *bottom, right;* it locks with a key on both sides. Remember, however, that should an emergency arise, you may have to get out quickly. To ensure a swift exit, always leave a key in the inside cylinder when you're at home. (Because of the danger of being trapped inside, some local fire codes prohibit double-cylinder locks; check the regulations in your area.)

Other effective locks are "rim-mounted" to a door's surface, like the version pictured *center, right.* You don't need to cut out a mortise for this type; simply bore a hole for the cylinder and attach the lock with screws.

If you've just moved into an older house, it's also a good idea to have a locksmith rekey all exterior door locks. More than a few people may still have keys to your home.

(continued)

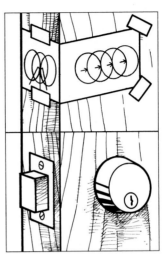

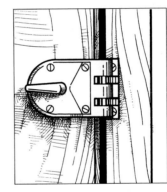

1 Mounting a dead bolt is similar to installing a knob set (see page 95). Just follow the instructions in the package you buy. A template also should be included; it will help you figure out where to drill holes for the lock. To make the job even simpler, buy a special kit for installing dead bolts, one that includes appropriate-size drill bits and a hole saw. As a final security precaution, install a protective plate around the cylinder to make it more difficult to get at the mechanism.

2 The rim-mounted vertical dead-bolt lock shown here discourages prying more than any other lock on the market. It, too, is easy to install. Position the lock 8 to 10 inches above the existing knob, and follow the accompanying instructions. Make sure that the screws you use to mount the hardware penetrate at least halfway into the door for a secure installation.

PROTECTING DOORS
(continued)

Door styles are almost as varied as windows. Some swing, some slide, some—like those on garages—roll up. Each calls for different hardware and a different security strategy.

All doors essential to your home's security should have double protection. With swinging doors, for example, a dead-bolt lock should be installed in addition to whatever other type is mortised in. A feature to look for when buying the dead bolt is a free-spinning, hardened steel pin within the bolt that resists sawing. A freely spinning ring surrounding the cylinder keeps an intruder's wrench from getting a secure grip.

When you're adding protective features throughout your home, remember to include your garage door. Many a homeowner has allowed his attached garage to become a hideout for the burglar's getaway vehicle.

No house is *entirely* safe from a thief who is bent on getting in. But strong doors and windows, buttressed by high-quality hardware, can go a long way toward foiling the plans of even the most determined intruders.

The photo on this page depicts a potpourri of products you can put on guard at your doors. The drawings *opposite* show how to install them.

latch cover

mortise dead bolt

high-security strike plate

peephole

rim-mounted vertical dead bolt

sliding door lock

barrel bolt

door pins

sliding door spacers

sliding door pin

1 Double doors—each of them—must be firmly secured, but in different ways. Treat the door receiving most of the traffic as you would any hinged exterior door. Fix the other in place by installing bar or barrel bolts at the top and bottom. Secure French doors with locking-type barrel bolts and a double-cylinder lock; otherwise, a thief could simply break out a pane or two.

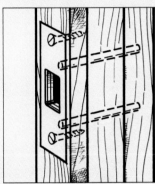

2 The best lock in the world won't be much help if its strike plate is weak or poorly installed. Replace a flimsy plate with a high-security model like the one shown here. Integral metal pins penetrate deeply into the jamb so the strike can't be pried loose. Or try a less expensive approach: Take out the screws in the existing plate, and insert new 2- or 2½-inch wood screws.

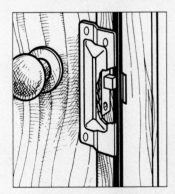

3 If a door swings to the outside, chances are its latch or bolt is not protected by a stop along the jamb. A custom metal guard plate can solve the problem. Fastened to the door with hard-to-get-at hardware, it prevents an intruder from hacksawing a bolt or jimmying the lock along the jamb. The cutaway drawing *at left* shows how the plate completely covers the door's latch.

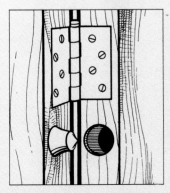

4 Occasionally, a break-in artist will pull the hinge pins free of their barrels and then work the door out of its opening. Prevent this from happening by installing tough metal door pins like the one shown here. The drawing shows the door in its open position. When the door is closed, the protruding steel pin fits into a hole in the door frame.

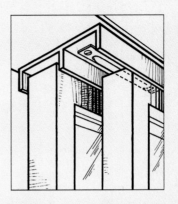

5 Some thieves just lift sliding glass doors (and windows) right out of their tracks. When the door is closed, these strong metal spacers won't let them get off the ground. With the sliding door open, position the metal plates (two per door) in the upper track, and screw them into predrilled holes. Remove the door for maintenance by sliding it to the full open position and lifting it out of the track.

6 If you want to prevent a burglar from being able to move a sliding glass door from side to side, insert a steel pin into a drilled hole through the inside door and partway into the outside door. Be sure to drill at least ⅝ inch away from the glass to avoid damaging glass which extends into the frame. Placing a broomstick in the bottom track also can foil an intruder.

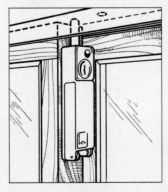

7 A heavy-duty lock, like the keyed version shown here, mounts with "one way" screws on the inside edge of the inside door (top or bottom). For extra security, a cover conceals the mounting screws in the locked position. This type of lock lets you keep the door locked and partly open at the same time, for ventilation and access for pets.

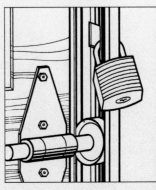

8 Don't forget your garage door. Make sure you're able to lock it as securely as any other exterior door. If yours rides on rollers like this one, protect it by hooking a padlock onto the track. Another convenient and secure solution is to install a remote control garage door opener.

ELECTRONIC SOLUTIONS

alarm

Reinforced windows and doors can hold most thieves at bay and send them away. If a burglar does break into your house, a reliable alarm system—with its shrill, loud sound—will alert the neighborhood, call the police for you, or notify personnel at a private security service.

Sound advice

But before you rush out to shop for an alarm system, consider some disadvantages. You may not care to deal with the constant annoyance of arming and disarming an alarm every time you leave and enter the house; this could be especially irksome in a home where many people come and go throughout the day. In addition, forgetful family members or guests not trained to use it properly can easily trip an alarm by accident.

On the other hand, protective alarms are good ways to provide additional security, especially in secluded or rural homes and especially if they're hooked up to notify neighbors and police when a break-in has occurred. In many locales, alarm systems also can be hooked up to a central station and monitored by trained security personnel.

What's it made of?

The simplest alarm systems contain three parts: a *sensor,* a *control unit,* and an *alarm.* When the sensor "spots" an intruder, it sends a signal to the control unit, which in turn sets off the alarm. You can buy these components in one self-contained unit or as individual parts that form a hardwire system (see the photo *at right* for examples of each).

Systems check

How much protection you get depends on the kind of elec-

tronic device and its position in or near the house. *Perimeter protection* systems are designed to monitor windows and doors; *interior protection* systems guard individual spots within your home. Generally, security specialists recommend a combination of both, but if your budget won't allow it, the most practical alternative is a comprehensive system that monitors ground-level entries to the house. Regardless of the one you select, it should be easy to control so you can avoid setting off false alarms.

It's also important to know something about the variety of sensors available on the market. Each works and responds in a characteristic way. To get an idea of the most common kinds you can buy, see the chart *opposite.* It briefly explains how they operate, how much space they safeguard, and what you should know about their distinctive advantages and disadvantages. As you're comparing them, keep in mind that some also can accommodate smoke and heat detectors.

Finally, choosing the alarm itself takes a little thought. *Local* alarms, the big noisemakers mentioned earlier, produce the sound of a loud siren or bell. (Some systems also cause floodlights to flash on and off.) They're a clear notice to neighbors—and occupants of the house—that a break-in is under way. To even the most brazen intruder, they're also a clear message that *now* is the time to get out.

Remote alarms—which may or may not make a noise at the scene—alert monitors at a central station or transmit a prerecorded message or signal to another person. Some security services send their own personnel, contact the police, or both.

magnetic sensor

control units

door alarm

ALARM SELECTOR

TYPE	HOW IT WORKS	COMMENTS

PERIMETER ALARMS

Single-Entry System

With the digital door-mounted model, an alarm sounds when a magnetic contact breaks with a frame-mounted magnetic switch. With another model, body electricity carried through the doorknob sets off the alarm.

Easy to install, both self-contained models provide inexpensive protection (under $50 each). However, both can be easily torn from doors and destroyed. Also, their alarms may not be heard on the outside.

Radio Frequency System (Wireless)

When current contact is broken, a magnetic sensor on the door or window sends a radio signal via a nearby wired transmitter to a receiver and alarm located elsewhere in the house.

Depending on the number of windows and doors to be protected, the price for magnetic sensors, transmitters, receiver, and alarm can run between $400 and $900 if professionals install the system. But with good instructions, a skilled homeowner can install it himself. One big disadvantage: A wireless system can set off a neighbor's alarm if they share the same frequency.

Conventional (Hard-Wire) System

An intruder opens a window or door wired with magnetic sensors. The movement disrupts current in the circuit, activating the receiver and sounding the alarm.

This system offers the most reliable protection, especially when tied into a central monitoring station. A variety of sensing devices, such as the pressure mat and photoelectric eye, can be hooked up to the overall system. However, because of the complicated wiring that's often necessary, professionals should do the installation. Needless to say, the price tag can get pretty high, depending on the amount of labor involved.

INTERIOR ALARMS

Electric Eye

An alarm sounds when an intruder breaks a visible beam of light stretching between an emitter and receiver.

Photoelectric protection can extend up to 100 feet across an entrance or room. The price is low—$50 to $100—and, with care, most homeowners can install the system on their own. However the beam is easily broken by accident, causing a false alarm. Plus, if a burglar sees it, he can simply get out of the way.

Infrared

A sensor monitors temperatures in a protected area. When an intruder's body heat raises the temperature in that spot, the alarm trips.

For a price of between $200 and $300, this system protects an area measuring up to 40x40 feet. Do-it-yourselfers can install it themselves, but they should remember to direct it over the heads of pets, whose body heat could set it off. Strong sunlight or a baseboard heater may also activate the alarm.

Detectors (Ultrasonic, Microwave)

Within a certain area, a sensor sends out and then receives silent sound waves. Any motion in that area disrupts the wave pattern and sets off the alarm.

Motion detectors cover a maximum of 25x25 feet. Averaging about $150 per alarm, self-contained units only need to be plugged in. Better models require professional help. Ultrasonics can be tripped by wind blowing through an open window, air conditioners, pets, and kids; microwaves, if not adjusted properly, may detect motion beyond a protected space and trigger a false alarm.

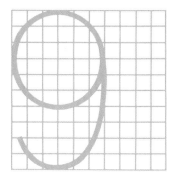

LET IN
MORE LIGHT

There's nothing like natural light to perk up your house. It's good for people, good for plants, and adds a cheeriness artificial light just can't match. Whether you brighten your home with window greenhouses, skylights, bumpouts, dormers, or other additions, few projects will be so rewarding. Properly built and placed, sun-loving additions also can act as passive solar collectors and reduce heating bills. This chapter shows some examples of additions and describes the particular advantages of each; they should help you decide just how and where to let more light into your house.

ADD A WINDOW GREENHOUSE

Finding the right niche for a ready-made greenhouse, like the unit *above*, is easy if you own an older home. With double-glazed glass in aluminum framing, the greenhouse fits nicely once the old window is removed. With a little help, set the unit into place and fasten it using lag screws. Finish the project by caulking to make it watertight.

Position, however, is important. Don't install a greenhouse facing directly south—sun rays will devastate most plants—or facing directly north—heat losses will send your energy bill soaring.

Lean-tos add room
Once the dead wall of a laundry room, the congenial gathering spot *opposite* came alive with the addition of a greenhouse unit called a lean-to. In effect a full greenhouse cut in half lengthwise, a ready-made lean-to is popular because it adds living space—for people as well as plants.

In cold climates, you'll probably want insulating shades to prevent heat loss at night. And any unit you select should have an adequate set of vents to let air in and heat out. However, only the largest units need extra warmth—and most will tap into your present heating and electrical systems.

GO THROUGH
THE ROOF

Light in unexpected places will bring new excitement to your house. A little creative thinking can turn low-light areas into pleasant work or entertainment centers. Going through the roof is one relatively inexpensive way to do it. Existing rafters often make additional framing unnecessary and the job uncomplicated. The two examples highlighted here may be just the answers to brightening up those dark and dreary areas in your home.

With the exposed rafters of the cathedral roof as framework, the half-glass ceiling in the home *opposite* not only adds a light-flooded cheeriness to the room, but it also creates the perception of increased space.

To begin, the owners removed the roofing, sheathing, insulation, and interior ceiling. They then placed double-glazed, patio-type door panels directly on the 2x12 rafters and sealed them against moisture, using silicone caulk and flashing on the peak side. To finish, they added ½-inch wood molding inside and out. Roll-up shades, concealed against a plank ceiling at the window tops, can be drawn to block out unwanted sun during the day or prevent heat loss at night.

The total effect is one of warmth, color, and depth provided by trees above and the yard beyond. A bonus is the passive solar heat that the new exposure brings into the house.

Open up eaves
Overhangs protect against heat gain on sunny exposures but cut out needed light on dark sides. The owners of the house *above* improved a drab kitchen by replacing a set of small, over-the-sink windows with counter-to-ceiling casements. Outside, they punched skylights into the eaves, giving the room a new source of overhead light. And because the ready-made units fit neatly between the rafters, no structural work was needed.

BRIGHTEN
YOUR ATTIC

Another way to go through the roof is to start at the top—in your attic. If you let the light in, it can be a bright and usable space. Most of the time, you can do the work yourself, barring any major structural changes. That means the price is right. To gain new work space, sleeping quarters, or even an entire office, redoing an attic is far less expensive than adding on to another part of your house.

A new ridgeline, dormers, and windows in the gable ends transformed a once-unused attic into a sun-filled bedroom *opposite*. To make the change, the owners bolstered the attic's entire roof structure and replaced the collar-tie beams with a 6x10 ridge beam supported by posts spaced along the attic's length. In the floor, new 2x12s were added to strengthen the joists. In addition, before installing drywall, the owners tightened up the room by placing fiberglass batts of insulation between the ceiling rafters.

Dormers on either side of the ridgeline not only provide more space but allow for the built-in storage this bedroom needs. An open, iron spiral staircase replaces old narrow stairs at the opposite end. To create a feeling of openness, gable-end windows let in more natural light and offer views of the cityscape.

Skylights brighten a dark attic

Rather than go to the expense of hiring a carpenter to frame in a costly dormer, the owner of the house *above* chose large skylights to lighten up his attic office. (Only one is shown here; the other is at the opposite end.) Both units are double-glazed and tight-fitting, yet open easily to release heat during the summer, an important consideration for any top-of-the-house remodeling.

Overall, the pair of bubble-type skylights and an intriguingly angled window in each gable end provide more than adequate light and fresh air to this formerly wasted space. For a step-by-step guide to installing a skylight of your own, see the next four pages.

ADD
A SKYLIGHT

Skylights are a versatile, economical way to beam natural light wherever you need it. You can run them the length of a long room or place them individually—a small one for the bath or twin units for the bedroom. Different glazings are available, too, to meet your needs. Pick milk-white acrylic for privacy, or add a diffuser panel. Try tinted glazings to reduce glare, or reflective ones to cut heat gain. Factory-built units are waterproof and easy to install. Here's how to do it.

To install a skylight, first check the framing in your attic. Note distances between rafters and ceiling joists —most units are designed to fit a 24-inch spacing or multiples of that dimension. For larger skylights, or if your roof has 16-inch on-center construction, you'll need to cut and tie off rafters and joists to accommodate the shaft.

When you're buying the skylight, also pick up some roofing felt, roofing cement, framing lumber for the opening, and ½- or ¾-inch plywood (either A-D or Medium Density Overlay for a smooth interior finish).

Next, decide whether to work from the inside out— framing the ceiling opening and building the shaft before cutting into the roof—or to start from the roof and work in, as shown *at right*. Whichever you choose, plan to get through the roof early in the day in case the weather changes.

To determine where the roof opening is, drive two nails from the attic side along the rafter and up through the sheathing. They'll serve as your marks for one side of the rectangle you'll cut from the outside. If intermediate framing members have to be cut out, either do it now or wait until you've opened the sheathing. To avoid sags or breaks in the rafters, brace them before you saw, then nail in framing crosspieces, as shown in the drawing *top right*.

Now you've begun what will turn out to be a fairly easy do-it-yourself project. (You will need at least one helper to get the unit to the roof and set it in place.) Just follow the sequence of photos and text on this page and pages 131-133. But before you do any cutting, check your house for errant wiring and water lines.

1 Up on the roof, you'll have to make room for the skylight. You can use an ordinary garden spade to pop up as many courses of shingles as necessary. Be sure to cut back the underlying roofing felt at least 8 inches around the opening you intend to use.

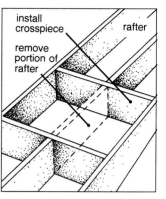

2 With a level as plumb guide, mark the four corners of the shaft opening on the now-exposed ceiling. Drive nails down through these points to serve as guides for a later cut, then frame the roof opening for support, as shown in the drawing *above, right*. In this project, one side of the opening ran along a rafter, so the builders had to fur in the other side and frame the top and bottom of the rectangle.

install crosspiece — rafter
remove portion of rafter

(Take care not to break the sometimes-fragile shingles when removing them.) Using the nails driven from the inside as reference points, measure, draw, and cut out the rectangle with a circular saw or saber saw.

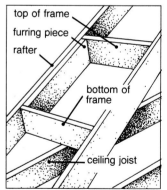

top of frame
furring piece
rafter
bottom of frame
ceiling joist

3 This skylight required a curb—a simple box made of 2x4s or 2x6s and placed around the roof opening to serve as a mounting base. If your unit calls for one, make its inside dimensions the same as the hole in the roof, and be sure the corners are square. Set it in a thick bed of roofing cement, as shown in the drawing *opposite*. Then toenail it down. Use another coat of cement to seal the curb's edge. For insurance, the crew here

4

3

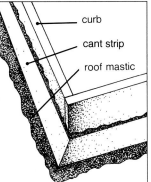

curb

cant strip

roof mastic

ripped 2x4s at a 45-degree angle to make the cant strips shown in the drawing *at left*. Carefully miter the corners, and apply a liberal amount of roofing cement to form a waterproof slope.

4 Next, finish off the roof opening by draping roofing felt over the curbing, as shown *above*. At the top and sides, overlap the felt with at least 12 inches of shingles; piece in a flap for the down-roof edge.

With cement and nails, secure the felt to the curbing, applying liberal amounts of cement at each place the felt overlaps.

Finally, reinstall the shingles. Working up-roof, nail them along the dotted lines, taking care to keep the courses even. When cutting shingles, make sure they butt tightly against the cant strips. When you've completed this step, temporarily nail the skylight in place.

(continued)

ADD
A SKYLIGHT

(continued)

Now you're ready for the second half of the installation—getting through the ceiling and constructing the plywood shaft.

You can install the shaft in a number of ways. If you want light directly under the roof opening, build a box that looks like the one in the drawing *below*. Or you can tilt the shaft so it's perpendicular to the roof and angles down through the attic, letting you offset the room and ceiling openings a little.

To create a lighted area inside that's bigger than the skylight itself, splay the sides of the shaft, somewhat like a pyramid with its top lopped off. To do this, the opening in your ceiling will have to be larger.

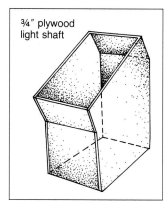

¾" plywood
light shaft

5 The next step is to open the ceiling. Lay plastic sheeting below because cutting through drywall or plaster creates a lot of dust. (Use a hand-operated keyhole saw; saber saws kick up too much of a mess.) And if you're sensitive to dust, wear a pair of goggles or a mask. You can support the drywall cutout with one hand while you're sawing, but plaster is heavier; hold it up with a 2x4 T-brace wedged against the floor.

When you've made the opening, you'll be flooded with light—but everything will still be rough around the edges.

As with the roof opening, frame and fur between joists, if necessary, making sure to support all cut ends.

Measuring for the shaft is tricky; it requires careful figuring. You might be wise to experiment with templates made from cardboard before cutting into the plywood. The shaft for this skylight ran from the ceiling to the top of the curb, which meant that the two end panels had to be angle-joined. The builders tested the fit first before setting up their cuts.

Once you've cut and test-fitted the shaft's components, install them one at a time. Or, assemble the entire unit and slide it into place. Fitting the pieces individually is probably easier, unless the space is very tight and you can't get to the shaft's outside corners to fasten them. If you *can* insert it as a unit without too much trouble, all the better: You'll be able to prime it first.

Join the shaft panels with wood glue and screws (the sheet-metal types bite better), and nail them to the rafters and joists all the way around. Be sure smooth faces point inward.

Then, make a trip to the attic to check your insulation. Batts and blankets should fit snugly around the base of the light shaft.

5

7

6

6 Fill every seam inside the shaft with paintable silicone caulk, then prime and paint, using a good exterior coating. Leakage usually isn't a problem, but condensation is, so seal the top edges, too.

7 To fasten down the skylight, first spread clean silicone sealant on the curb's top edge, and press the unit into place. Secure it to the curb with wood screws. Skylights

8

that don't need curbs generally have flashing attached to their frames. Tuck it under the top and sides of the roofing, but let it overlap down-roof shingles.

8 The ceiling opening in this project was trimmed with 2¼-inch stock molding, mitered at the corners and painted to blend. To reduce heat loss, add a sheet of white acrylic plastic, or use a hinged or sliding shutter panel.

LET IN MORE LIGHT

ADD A BUMP-OUT

Want to combine a quiet nook for reading with a badly needed window on the world? Adding a bump-out to a bedroom, living room, or kitchen is one sensible way to gain more light and space. Whether it takes the shape of a dormer or bay, or is part of a larger addition, the results are the same: warm, natural light and those few extra feet of living space you've always wanted.

Part of the second-story addition to a single-story ranch house, the light-filled window seat *opposite* is an area for reading and relaxing in a new master bedroom. The dramatic, yet pleasing, change in the original structure features the same siding and roofing materials and follows the home's original lines. As a result, the bay extension blends in nicely with the entry *above*.

When the homeowners planned this addition, they incorporated a peaceful den into the bedroom's design so they could enjoy quiet times away from the family bustle. The cozy 6x2½-foot window seat is part of that den; it not only makes a sunny reading nook but is also a great spot to watch the changing seasons in the wooded yard. The nook's lowered ceiling follows the roof line of the bay extension and gives it a self-contained feeling. Windows on each of the three sides catch sun all afternoon. The large angular ones are fixed, but the smaller side windows swing out so air can enter the room.

A bay like this is easily bumped-out from an existing wall and supported by cantilevering out from the floor joists. As noted before, the bump-out shown here is part of an entire second-floor addition; for that reason, the roof of the bay is an integral part of the new roof line.

If you want to add a bump-out and nothing more to a room, you'll either have to tie the new roof into the old or top off the addition with its own roof. In either case, plan it so you get the best view and most light possible.

CANTILEVER
OUT
WITH A BAY

Filling your house with light doesn't always have to mean a major overhaul or huge addition. Look for areas you can easily extend by poking out from existing joists. Most homes have a number of likely spots: a screened porch, entry, or blank wall. Pick one, and use it as a bright new place for plants, a sunny nook for reading, or a delightful backdrop for family meals. In the process, you may even add a little solar heat to your house.

The pair of cantilevered greenhouse bump-outs shown *opposite* and *above* are part of a converted porch, and are areas that now provide extra dining space and sunlight for a small and once-dreary kitchen.

Cantilevering is simply the technique of extending beams or joists beyond a support member. How far you can extend a cantilever is directly related to the size of the beams, joists, and other support members in your house. Usually, cantilevered bays and other projections can extend no more than a few feet. But the big advantage of this building technique is a matter of dollars and cents: You don't need expensive foundation work, nor must you add supporting columns or posts.

Each of the tandem greenhouses, measuring about 7 feet high and 10 feet across, was cantilevered from the joists of the old porch floor. Because the old floor joists in this house ended at the exterior wall, the owners attached new 2x8-inch joists for the extension. (To ensure stability and support, anchor the new joists to existing ones at least 2 feet inside the old wall, depending on the depth of your bump-out.)

The framework for the double-glazed glass is made of 4x4 posts, which join 4x4 rafters for a well-balanced look that matches the home's traditional architecture. The units extend only about a foot from the original wall. Although this

distance isn't very much, before beginning your own project, check local building codes to see how close you can approach the lot lines.

Functional as well as attractive, these greenhouse bays feature floors with gravel-filled pans and a drain hole for carrying excess water directly outside. For a break on your fuel bill, you could easily turn them into passive solar collectors by installing heat-saturating brick and sand in lieu of the water-catching gravel, and then shading the windows at night to prevent heat loss. To keep plant foliage from sunburning, the greenhouses are fitted with smoked glass. On both sides of each unit are small ventilating windows to dissipate heat and moisture, a must for any installation of this type.

CONNECT WITH OUTDOOR LIVING

Whether you live in the heart of a city or on a wooded country lot, sunshine and fresh air can be constant guests in your home. By adding expanses of glass, you let nature in, blending it with the way you live and the things you own. In the process, rooms seem—quite naturally— roomier than they are.

A pair of sliding glass patio doors and walls of windows brings the outside in for the homeowners who converted their attic *opposite, above* to enjoyable living space. Outside, a patio built of wood planks enhances the view even more, and provides a secluded spot to lie in the sun.

In this "open dormer," the owners set in double-glazed doors to give an illusion of space and to let in as much light as possible. To complete the wall of glass, they separated the standard 6-foot-wide doors with a floor-to-ceiling window. Whenever they want ventilation, they simply open the doors, as well as swing-out windows at each end of the patio. Triangular windows in each gable, visible at the end of the hall, carry out the ceiling lines and provide extra lighting.

Installing glass walls is often complicated because most studs have to be removed and replaced by double headers for support. In this remodeling, the framed-glass panel between the sliding doors is more than enough to support the roof. If you're not sure how wide a glass wall can be, consult a professional, rather than risk sagging roofs or walls.

Sunny-side up

The countryside surrounding the house *opposite, below* is definitely part of the great indoors. Wide expanses of glass along the south side brighten, lighten, and warm the house, while providing panoramic views of the valley. In summer, the sliding glass doors open the living room to the deck and bring the two areas together. A skylight, just above the half-height wall, bathes the center of the room with light.

Originally, the owners built this house to take advantage of an excellent site for passive solar energy. Although the house doesn't have a complete solar heating system, all that glass along the south side picks up a lot of warmth. In summer, the roof overhangs stop the windows from adding too much sun, and cross ventilation from the other side of the house keeps the interior cool. Undue heat loss in colder weather is prevented by double-glazed glass and insulating shades.

The rewards for using so much glass are plain to see. The house has an open, airy atmosphere, with the outdoors becoming a visual extension of interior space. And sliding glass doors throughout provide easy access to the decks and yard.

Because the house was built to accommodate large areas of glass, it has the structural features necessary to stand up to them. The extra-wide sliding glass door has a thicker than normal header above the opening, as does the framing for the picture windows. Note, too, the space between the top of the doors and the ceiling— it indicates sound support.

Selecting a site—to get the most sun and the best view— was a top priority for this family. Gaining passive solar heat is only feasible if a bank of glass is within 30 degrees of due south, so be sure to take siting into consideration in your building or remodeling plans. Even homes built in extreme northern latitudes can take advantage of sunny exposures. And today's thermal glass and insulating technology make it possible to enjoy the best of both worlds year-round.

HOW ENERGY EFFICIENT ARE SLIDING GLASS DOORS?

Compared to ordinary-size windows, large glass patio doors are bound to lose heat. However, their value as solar collectors and light transmitters can more than offset the loss. Even so, keep the following points in mind when you're thinking about installing sliding glass doors:

• *Where will they be installed?* The south side is best, or within 30 degrees of south. North is by far the worst.

• *Is the glass double-glazed?* Double-glazing (two thicknesses of glass with air space between) cuts heat loss by 50 percent or more. Triple-glazing reduces the loss by two-thirds.

• *Will the sash conduct heat?* Wood sash and framing make better insulators than metal.

• *Who'll do the job?* The work must be done carefully: A tight-fitting installation is the best insurance against heat loss. Replacing insulation around the door, caulking, and weather stripping are necessary.

• *Can you use draperies?* Insulating draperies or shades, made to fit inside the casing, cut down on heat loss and trap air leaks.

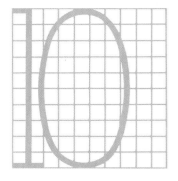

REPAIRING AND MAINTAINING WINDOWS AND DOORS

Few of your home's components work harder than doors and windows. Countless openings and closings, variations in humidity and temperature, not to mention the normal wear and tear of just being there, eventually take their toll. Fortunately, if you don't let your repair and maintenance list get too lengthy, you can handle each malady or maintenance chore promptly and without too much effort.

HOW TO PAINT WINDOWS AND DOORS

Anyone *can* do a good job of renewing doors and windows with paint, but not everyone *does*.

Painting windows and doors properly calls for two important ingredients—patience and a steady hand. Patience is required to prepare surfaces carefully, and a steady hand is necessary to paint narrow window and door trim and to keep a neat edge between woodwork and walls.

Choose a good alkyd paint for your project. You'll need solvent to clean up, but the tough, durable surface alkyd produces is well worth the extra effort. Keep in mind, too, that the glossier the finish, the more durable and easier to clean it will be.

Prep work

Your paint project will go much more smoothly if you prepare the surfaces to be painted, as shown in the drawings *below*. Inspect each door or window for peeling paint. Scrape away any you find with a wire brush or a putty knife. Sand the rough edges and prime any bare spots. Next, remove or mask around all door or window hardware. Also mask around window muntins unless you have a very steady hand. Finally, lay down drop cloths to protect floors and furnishings.

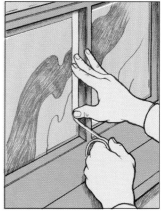

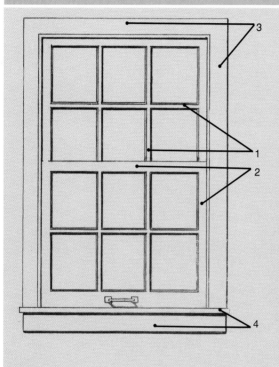

As illustrated *at left*, the basic idea when painting windows and doors is to work from the inside out. On double-hung windows, for example, you should start with the muntins, then paint the sashes, casing, sill, and apron, in that order. Be sure to have the windows in the open position; otherwise, you run the risk of painting them shut. If your windows slide in wooden channels, push both sashes to the lower half of the window and paint the upper side jambs; when paint has dried, push both windows up and paint the lower jambs. Rub the channels with paraffin or spray them with silicone after paint has dried fully. Leave metal channels unpainted. Wipe up spills with a solvent-moistened rag as soon as they occur. (See *below* for additional painting and clean-up tips.)

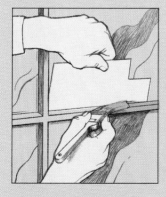

If your hand is steady, paint without aids; if not, mask the area you don't want to paint or use a paint shield. A sash brush works well when painting window muntins.

Accidents will happen. When they do, wipe them up immediately. For spatters that have already set, carefully chip off the paint with a scraper.

Remove masking tape as soon as you have finished painting the immediate area. Wait too long, and you risk pulling off the new paint along with the tape.

You can best clean paint from window glass by first letting it dry, then using a scraper to cut off the excess. Be careful not to nick the wood, though.

REPAIRING
SHADES AND BLINDS

Like anything mechanical, blinds and shades don't work perfectly all the time. Resist the temptation to replace them whenever something goes wrong—at least until you try to find—and fix—the problem yourself.

With *shades,* you can right most wrongs in a matter of minutes. If the shade goes up with a bang, there's too much tension on the spring. To reduce it, take down the shade, unroll it a few inches, and replace it. If the shade goes up too slowly, you need to increase the tension. Take down the shade and turn the end pin clockwise a couple of revolutions.

Maybe the shade won't catch. Check for a bent or worn bracket, and make sure the ratchet is holding. You generally can straighten a bracket, but if the ratchet's shot, you'll have to replace the roller.

And if your shades bind or fall down, check the clearance between the brackets and the roller. Adjust as necessary.

Venetian blinds, although more complex in design than shades, aren't difficult to fix either. If problems develop, first study the drawing *at right* to familiarize yourself with your blinds' components. The one shown is a mini-slat type. If yours are older, they'll have cloth ladders rather than cords, and a tilt cord instead of a wand. Mechanically, both types are quite similar.

Next, try to locate the source of the problem. If the tilting mechanism balks, you may have dirt or cord threads in the worm gear. If the blind won't go up or down, check for a broken cord, or on older types, one that's jumped a pulley. Should you find frayed or broken cords, replace them as shown *opposite.*

HOW THEY WORK

ANATOMY OF A ROLLER SHADE

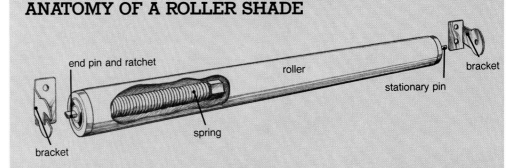

end pin and ratchet

roller

bracket

stationary pin

spring

bracket

ANATOMY OF A VENETIAN BLIND

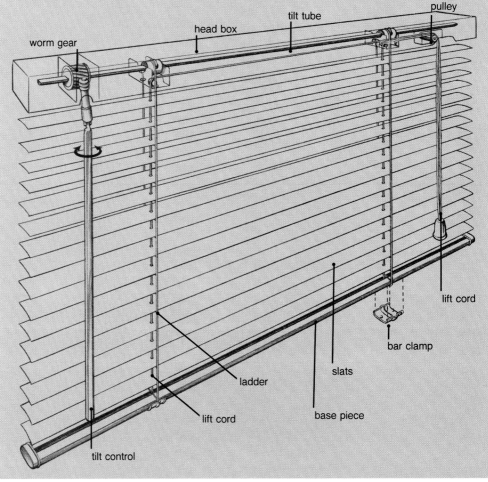

worm gear

head box

tilt tube

pulley

ladder

lift cord

slats

bar clamp

base piece

lift cord

tilt control

REPLACING LADDERS AND CORDS

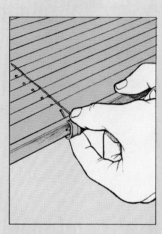

1 Start by removing the blind from the window. Then lay it on a flat surface and remove the clamps from the underside of the base piece. With the type shown, release the clamps from inside the base piece with a pointed object. Clamps on older metal types snap off; blinds with wooden base pieces typically don't have clamps.

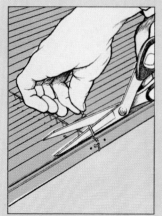

2 Now, either untie or snip off the two lift cords attached to the blind's base piece. To remove the lift cords, simply pull on the cords as if you were raising the blind. With this done, you can now remove the slats from the ladders if you have to replace the ladders. Leave the slats in place if you're replacing only the lift cords.

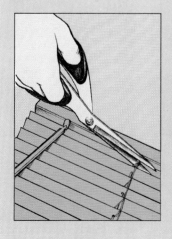

3 To remove ladders from the newer-style blinds, just snip the cords near the base piece and the head box. Be sure to remove the remaining portion of the cords still inside. With the older-style blinds, first pull the ladders loose from the base piece. On top, you'll find a hairpinlike clip holding each tape to the tilt tube. Remove these clips to completely free the ladder.

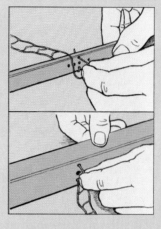

4 To install new ladders, thread the cords through the holes in the base piece and head box, as shown *at left*. (With older blinds, staple the bottom of the new ladder to the underside of the base piece, and attach the upper portion to the head box via the hairpinlike clips.)

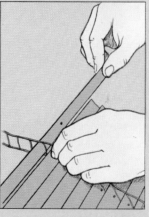

5 Once the ladders are securely fastened at top and bottom, extend the ladders and slip a slat into each of the openings. Be sure to insert them with the crowned side facing up. This procedure is exactly the same regardless of the type blind you have.

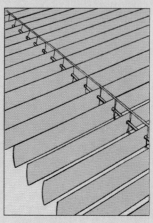

6 To complete the project, thread the two ends of the lift cord up through the large opening in the bottom of the head box, down through the small holes above each of the ladders, and through the openings in the slats. Be sure to weave the cord on alternate sides of the rungs. Then tie the cords to the base piece. If your blinds have a tilt cord, thread a new cord over the gear and other pulleys; replace the tassels.

REPLACING
BROKEN GLASS

In the past, when an errant baseball found its way into a window, or a rapid temperature change fractured a pane, many people simply called in a local handyman and had him make the repair. But things have changed today. Even if you can locate someone to help you out, the cost for the repairs can be considerable.

With know-how, anyone can replace a broken pane. On this page and pages 145 and 146, we show you how to deal with both wood-frame and metal-frame windows. And on page 146, you can learn how to cut the glass yourself. (The procedures we show apply to windows with single-pane glass in them. Some newer, energy-efficient windows come with double or triple glazing. If one of these needs repair, you'll need to contact a dealer for professional help.)

For the task at hand, however, in addition to replacement glass cut to the correct size, you'll need push-type glazier's points and glazing compound. To figure the size of pane you need, measure the length and width of the opening and subtract ⅛ inch from each dimension. You can buy standard replacement glass at some hardware stores and all glass companies.

CAUTION: Whenever you handle or cut glass, be very careful. Always wear gloves to protect your hands, because both glass shards and the edges of new glass frequently are sharp.

(continued)

REGLAZING WOOD-FRAME WINDOWS

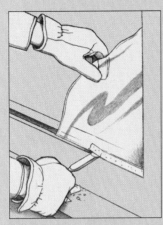

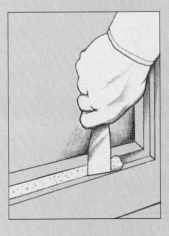

1 Removing a window sash can be quite time-consuming, so if possible, make the repair with the window in place. Start by removing any glass shards, then chip off any glazing compound with a putty knife. (If any of it won't budge, you may have to heat it with a soldering iron.) To enable the new compound to adhere better, use a scraper to rough up the base of the recess that the new glass will rest in.

2 If you haven't already done so, measure the length and width of the opening to determine the size of pane needed. Don't forget to subtract ⅛ inch from each dimension.

To prepare the recess for the glazing compound, prime it with linseed oil, turpentine, or oil-base paint. If you don't take the time to do this, the untreated wood will draw oil from the glazing compound and poor adhesion will result.

3 Prior to inserting the new glass, spread a ⅛-inch bead of glazing compound along the base of the recess. Doing this helps create a seal and provides a cushion on which the glass rests. Now, carefully position the glass; be sure to apply enough (but not too much) pressure to the pane so the glazing compound spreads.

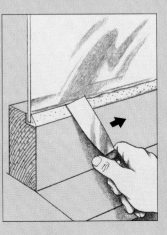

4 Once the glass is firmly in place, secure it by pressing several glazier's points along each edge of the glass into the surrounding sash. Generally, a putty knife is the best tool to use for this operation. Be sure when doing this that you don't press too hard against the glass.

5 Take some glazing compound out of its container and shape it into a ¼-inch rope. Press the compound into place, as shown *at left,* making sure that it adheres to both the glass and the sash.

6 Using a putty knife angled to ensure adequate drainage away from the glass, bevel the compound as shown. If you have trouble with the compound sticking to the knife, wet the blade with turpentine or linseed oil.

Before painting the compound, give it about a week to cure. When painting, allow the paint to overlap the glass by 1/16 inch to help seal the joint between the glass and the compound.

REGLAZING METAL-FRAME WINDOWS

With metal-frame windows, the reglazing procedure depends on the construction of the frame. Many basement windows, for example, have a *one-piece frame.* With these, the glass is held in place with either spring clips and glazing compound or a vinyl spline. Other windows have *knock-apart frames* that you disassemble in one of the ways shown *at right*.

To reglaze one-piece-frame windows, chip away the glazing compound and remove the spring clips or pry out the spline with a screwdriver. Then, clean the channel in which the glass fits.

For windows with spring clips, lay a bead of compound along the flange the glass rests on, then position the glass, insert the clips, and fill the gap between the frame and glass with glazing compound. If the window has vinyl splines, insert the glass into the opening and reinsert the spline, using the screwdriver.

The procedure for windows with knock-apart frames depends on the type. If the frames have screws, simply remove them, insert new glass, and reinsert the screws. If the frames have spring clips, pop them off, install new glass, and refit the clips.

If your windows have internal L-brackets dimpled in place at their corners, release them by drilling out the dimples. Then, make new dimples with an awl to hold the brackets in place.

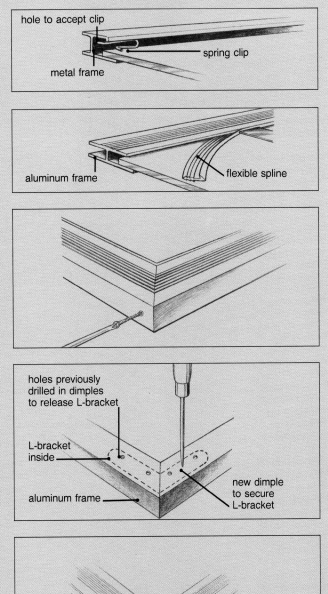

hole to accept clip
spring clip
metal frame

aluminum frame
flexible spline

holes previously drilled in dimples to release L-bracket
L-bracket inside
aluminum frame
new dimple to secure L-bracket

slot
spring clip

REPLACING BROKEN GLASS

(continued)

HOW TO CUT GLASS

1 Using a measuring rule and a framing square, determine the cutoff line. (Don't forget to make the pane ⅛ inch shorter and narrower than the size of the opening.) Then, using the framing square as a straightedge, score the glass with a glass cutter. Press hard on the cutter, and make only one pass over the glass.

2 To fracture the glass, place the score line directly above an object that will allow you to exert some downward pressure on the glass. A length of galvanized pipe was used here. Then, with one gloved hand on either side of the score line, snap the glass in two.

3 Generally, you'll get a clean break. When you don't, it's because the glass cutter failed to score the surface adequately. Often, you can salvage a piece with a jagged edge by using nippers, pliers, or another clamping tool, as shown *at left*. Be very careful when performing this operation; glass can be treacherous.

HOW TO CLEAN GLASS

Knowing how to clean glass correctly will save you time and result in clear, streak-free windows.

Polish them with lint-free cloths, newspapers, or a chamois—or master the knack of manipulating a squeegee the way the pros do.

Start by getting organized. If possible, enlist a helper, then get two of everything you need so you both can work at the same time on the same window; one inside, one out. Besides polishers or a squeegee, you'll need window cleaner (or an ammonia and water solution), trisodium phosphate (TSP) and water solution, a scouring brush, and one or more sturdy stepladders. (If you're dealing with second-story windows, you may want to consider having a professional do the outsides for you.)

Before attempting to clean the glass panes, scrub the frame surrounding them (if necessary) with the TSP/water solution. Let it set for awhile, then rinse the frame with a clean, damp cloth.

Now, spray or brush on the window cleaner, then wipe the window with a cloth, chamois, or wadded-up newspaper. (With newspapers, when one gets too wet, simply toss it and use another ball.) If you can still detect smudges or streaks, repeat the process.

Working a squeegee

It takes awhile to learn the correct way to squeegee, especially with large expanses of glass. Once you learn how, though, you can wipe down windows in about half the time it takes to polish them, and you don't need to lug around a lot of cloths or newspapers.

If your windows have multiple panes, purchase a squeegee one pane wide. Then you can clear each with a single pass. Brush or sponge on window cleaning solution (the wetter the better) and scrub off dirt. Now hold the squeegee firmly against the glass and draw it down in a single stroke.

The main thing to keep in mind is that you must wipe off the squeegee after each pass. The rubber blade must be clean and dry to do its work. With multi-paned windows, work from top to bottom, also wiping off the muntin at the bottom of each pane before squeegeeing the pane below.

With bigger windows, you'll need to make several overlapping passes, again wiping off the blade after each. If you get streaks where the passes overlap, wipe them away with a soft, clean cloth. Pros end each downward stroke by looping up again, like drawing a giant J. This keeps excess water from spilling over the bottom of the frame. Then they end with a single horizontal pass along the bottom edge of the glass.

REPAIRING DOUBLE-HUNG WINDOWS

REPLACING CORDS

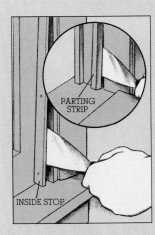

1 To gain access to a window's sash cords, you have to remove the inside stop from both sides of the sash. And if the upper sash needs attention, the parting stops must come off, too. Carefully pry the stops away from the jambs with a wide-bladed putty knife. Then lift the sash clear of the stool and swing it out.

PARTING STRIP

INSIDE STOP

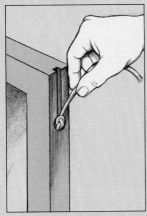

2 With the sash free from the window, you can now remove the sash cord from the keyed slot in its side. Then, remove the access panel if your windows have them. Inside you'll be able to get at and remove the sash weight. No access panels? Then you'll have to remove the casing and the wall material behind it to get at the weight.

3 Thread the new sash cord over the pulley and down into the sash weight cavity until it appears at the access panel. Tie the sash weight to the sash cord, then put the weight back into the cavity. Knot the other end of the sash cord at a point that will permit the weight to hang 3 inches above the sill when the sash is fully raised. Return the sash to its place and nail the stops to the jambs.

As shown *below,* there's much more going on inside a double-hung window than you might think. Of particular note from a repair standpoint are the channels in which the sashes move up and down, and the sash weights and pulleys on either side of each sash. (Newer double-hung windows have spring balance devices rather than sash weights, but both allow the windows to raise and lower with minimal effort.)

When double-hung windows fail to operate properly, one of three problems probably exists. If the window won't budge, either it's been painted shut or one of the stop moldings has warped. If, on the other hand, the window won't stay open or closed, a sash cord has probably broken or a spring balance must be adjusted or replaced.

Sashes that have been painted shut will yield to pressure from a putty knife or a pry bar. If the sash is binding between its stops, tap along their length with a wooden block to separate them. *(continued)*

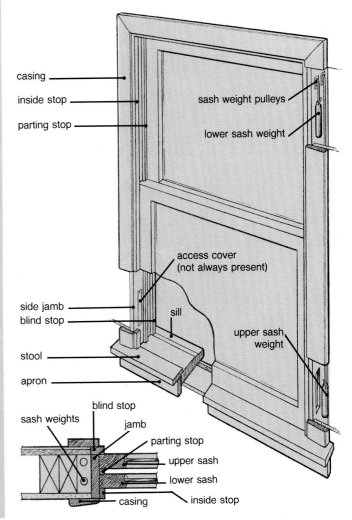

casing

inside stop

parting stop

sash weight pulleys

lower sash weight

access cover (not always present)

side jamb

blind stop

stool

apron

sill

upper sash weight

sash weights

blind stop

jamb

parting stop

upper sash

lower sash

casing

inside stop

REPAIRING DOUBLE-HUNG WINDOWS

(continued)

ADJUSTING BALANCES

1 Sometimes, when a window fitted with spring balances has remained closed for an extended period of time, its springs weaken. If they have, the window won't stay open as it should. To correct this situation, first close the window, then remove the screw holding the balance tube to the jamb. Make sure to keep the tube from rotating counterclockwise and losing still more tension.

2 Now rotate the tube three or four revolutions in a clockwise direction to tighten the spring inside the tube. Reposition the tube against the jamb and secure the tube by driving the screw into the jamb. Repeat this same procedure with the sash's other balance.

REPLACING BALANCES

1 Occasionally, a spring or a spiral twist rod inside the balance tube breaks. When this happens, you need to replace the entire assembly. Start by removing the screw holding the balance tube to the window jamb. Let the balance unwind fully, then remove the stops holding the window in place. (With some brands, the jambs are spring-loaded, so just force the sash to one side to release it.)

2 With windows that don't have spring-loaded jambs, you'll have to pry out the sash with a pry bar or other suitable tool. As you do so, be sure that you don't damage the surrounding woodwork.

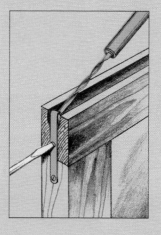

3 Once you've freed the sash, turn it onto its side and remove the screws holding the balance tube to the sash. Position the new assembly in its channel, then fasten it to the sash as before. Reinstall the sash in the window, replace the stops if necessary, increase tension on the balance by rotating it clockwise several times, and fasten the tube to the jamb.

REPAIRING
AND REPLACING
SCREENING

Window screening, when in good repair, lets you reap the benefits of refreshing outside air without worrying about insects invading the premises. But if even a small hole or tear develops, it won't take flying or crawling pests long to find their way into your home.

If you have only a small tear, one quick, easy way to repair it—in either fiber-glass or metal screening—is with clear silicone glue. Just dab it on over the tear and let the glue set.

You may have to apply several coats to close the hole.

Metal screening also responds well to "darning" with strands of scrap screening. Unravel a strand or two and, using a sewing needle, weave the strands into the undamaged screen.

With larger holes, the preceding repair tactics won't get the job done. But don't buy another screen until you consider the possibility of applying a patch. You may be able to save both time and money.

To make a repair of this type in metal screening, first square off the hole's edges with tin snips. Then cut a piece of scrap screening that's about 2 inches larger than the damaged area. Unravel a couple of the patch's strands on each side and bend them at a 90-degree angle. Fit the patch over the opening and insert the strands through the screening. Once satisfied with the patch's position, bend the wires over to secure it.

You also can apply a similar technique to mending fiber-glass screening. Again, square off the damaged area, cut an oversized patch from scrap material, and affix it with clear silicone glue.

Good as these procedures are, they won't handle major damage to screens. For information about replacing screening material in metal and in wooden frames, see *below* and on the following page.

(continued)

REPLACING METAL-FRAME SCREENING

1 Start by laying the screen on a worktable or other flat surface. Metal-framed screens are held in place by a vinyl spline that fits into a channel that runs the entire perimeter of the frame. To remove the spline, insert the tip of a flat-bladed screwdriver into the channel and pry up on it. Once you get it started, it's a simple matter to pull the remainder out of the channel.

2 Separate the damaged screening from the frame. And after squaring-up the frame, lay a piece of replacement screening over the frame. Using a pair of tin snips, cut a slightly oversize piece of material (generally, cutting it to the same dimensions as the frame's outside measurements works well).

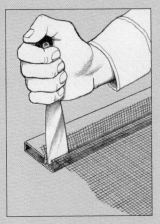

3 Place the new screening over the opening in the frame and, using a putty knife, awl, or other suitable tool, crease the screening down into the channel along one side. This is the edge of the screening you'll be stretching against first.

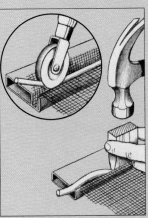

4 Now reinsert the spline using a hammer and wooden block or a screening tool. Then have someone pull the screening taut while you drive a second spline into the opposite channel. Start either of the two remaining sides of the screen as before and repeat the stretching process. Finish the project by trimming the excess screening.

REPAIRING AND REPLACING SCREENING

(continued)

REPLACING WOOD-FRAME SCREENING

1 In wood-frame screens, the screening is held in tension by staples that are driven all along the perimeter of the sash. But to get at them you must first remove the screen molding, which neatly conceals the staples and the raw edges of the screening. To do this, gently pry up each strip, using a putty knife. Be very careful, though. With age the molding gets quite brittle.

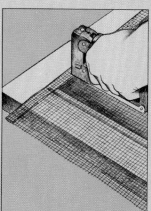

2 Remove the staples holding the screening to the sash and discard the old screening. Unroll a length of replacement screening and cut a piece that is several inches wider and at least 12 inches longer than the frame. Fold over the top edge of the screening about ½ inch and staple this hemmed double layer to the sash as shown, working out from the center to the edges.

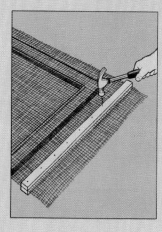

3 To ensure an adequate amount of tension on the screening, it's a good idea to fashion a makeshift "stretcher" of a pair of 1x2s. Cut two 1x2s as long as the window is wide, then nail one of them to the floor. Position the screen and sash as shown, with the excess screening overlapping the nailed-down 1x2. Nail a second 1x2 to the one already in place.

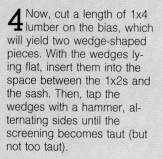

4 Now, cut a length of 1x4 lumber on the bias, which will yield two wedge-shaped pieces. With the wedges lying flat, insert them into the space between the 1x2s and the sash. Then, tap the wedges with a hammer, alternating sides until the screening becomes taut (but not too taut).

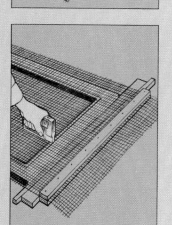

5 Staple the bottom edge of the screening in place, again working from the center outward to each edge. For the sides, pull the fabric taut and staple from the center outward, smoothing the mesh as you go. Trim the excess screening from the frame with a utility knife and replace the molding.

REPAIRING DOORS

oors that squeak or don't open and close properly are a source of daily irritation and, in some cases, can compromise the security and energy efficiency of your home.

Below and on the next page, we show you how to make several hinged door repairs. For tips on keeping patio and bypass doors sliding smoothly, read on.

Patio doors
These heavy, glass exterior doors slide on rollers mounted on the bottom of the doorframe. Most problems are caused by dirt that collects in the track in which the door slides. That's why keeping the track clean is a necessity. After each cleaning, puff powdered graphite onto the track or apply paraffin to keep the door running smoothly.

A binding door can also result from a bent track. Often, you can solve this problem by tapping out the bend with a hammer and wooden block.

For a door that's not sliding squarely on its rollers, check to see if the door's movable sash is square with the track. If it appears out of alignment, adjust the rollers up or down by locating the access plug near the bottom of the door. Turn the plug's screw clockwise to raise the rollers; counterclockwise to lower them.

Bypass doors
These lightweight wooden interior doors hang from rollers that slide in a track mounted at the top of the frame. When these act up, you can bet that one of three things has happened. The screws holding the roller brackets may have come loose, one of the rollers may have jumped the track, or the floor guides may have become bent. Tightening the screws holding the roller brackets in place, lifting the roller back on track again, and straightening or replacing the floor guides will get the problem door rolling properly again.

FREEING A BINDING HINGED DOOR

1 With a door that's binding near the top or bottom of the latch edge, first check to make sure the screws holding the hinges to the jamb are tight. If they are, shimming out one of the hinges should correct the situation. (Note: Shim the top hinge to free a bind near the bottom; the bottom hinge for binds near the top.) Use cardboard as the shim material, and place it behind the hinge leaf connected to the jamb.

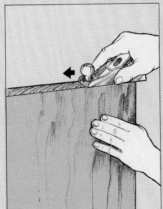

2 Shimming as shown *above, left* will solve a bind at a door's edge but may cause the top or bottom to bind. If this happens, close the door as far as possible and determine where the bind is occurring. Scribe a light mark on the door to highlight the high spots. If the bind is at the top, open the door partway and plane down the high spots. Be sure to work from the edges of the door to the center to avoid splintering end grain.

3 If it turns out that you have to remove material from the hinge or bottom edges, you'll need to take the door down for planing. To do this, first close the door as far as possible, then work a pry bar between each hinge pin and the top of the hinge, and tap it loose with a hammer. Replace each of the pins in the hinge leaf fastened to the jamb immediately after taking down the door, so you don't lose it.

4 Once you have the door down, stand it on edge, place the door so one end of it is in a corner, and straddle the other end. This should provide enough stability so that you can plane down the high spots. If you're planing the bottom of the door, you'll want to use a block plane. Otherwise, use a jack plane to remove the excess wood. Remember to plane from the ends to the center to avoid splitting the wood.

REPAIRING DOORS
(continued)

CURING HINGE ILLS

1 Over time, the screws holding a door's hinges can work loose. You may be able to simply retighten the screws, but often you'll have to use one of two other techniques. If the holes in the hinge leaves will accept larger-diameter screws, use them. If not, drill out existing holes, insert ¼-inch glue-coated wooden dowels, drill pilot holes, and drive the screws into the dowels.

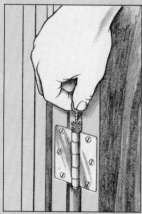

2 To get the squeaks out of your doors, pry up the hinge pins, then squirt some lubricating oil into the barrel. Open and close the door several times to allow the oil to work its way down. If that doesn't work, open the door fully, drive a shim under the hinge side of the door, and remove the hinge pins one at a time. Clean the barrel with a small wire brush.

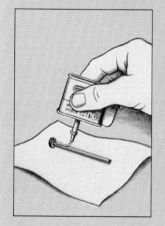

3 While you have each hinge pin out, inspect it for rust buildup. If the pin is severely rusted, remove the rust by polishing the pin with a grinder or applying a rust-removing solution. Even if you don't spot any rust, be sure to lay on a light coat of oil, as shown, to keep things moving.

STRIKE/LATCH REPAIRS

1 A latch and strike plate that don't quite match up will prevent any door from closing the way it should. To solve the problem, first check to see which edge of the strike the latch is hitting. If only a minor adjustment is necessary, you can remove the strike, put it in a vise, and file down the offending edge. Or lengthen the strike mortise and move the strike up or down as needed for a correct fit.

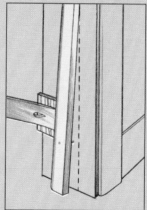

2 Sometimes, though, a door doesn't close far enough for the latch to engage the strike. Here, your only alternative is to move the door's stop molding. (This technique also works well for doors that rattle while closed.) Start by carefully prying off the stop molding from the jambs. Place a scrap of wood between the pry bar and the jamb to prevent damage.

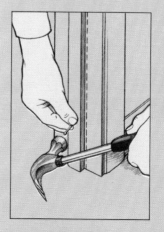

3 Once you have removed the stop molding, close the door and make a line on the jamb to indicate where the edge of the stop will be. Then, reposition the molding along the line you've drawn. Finish by painting or staining the area left exposed when you moved the molding.

A GLOSSARY OF WINDOW AND DOOR TERMS

Throughout this book, we've defined terms that are important for understanding the doors and windows at your house. This glossary makes it easier to look up specific items. For more information, check the index for pages where terms are illustrated or discussed in more detail.

Apron. Interior trim below the window sill. It covers the gap between the sill and the adjoining wall material.

Austrian shade. A fabric shade that raises and lowers in scallops by means of a series of tapes to which rings, threaded with cord, are attached.

Awning window. A window whose sash is hinged at the top and tilts outward. It opens and closes by means of a scissors- or hinge-type cranking system.

Balloon shade. Cousin to the Roman shade, this fabric window treatment raises with a soft, poufed bottom edge. It operates by means of a series of tapes with rings through which cords are threaded.

Bay window. A multi-sash type that extends outward beyond the plane of the adjoining wall.

Bifold door. A pair of solid or hollow-core panels hinged together. One pivots on fixed pins; the other slides along a track.

Bow window. Similar to a bay window, except that the sides curve rather than extend at an angle.

Bypass doors. A pair of doors that roll along an overhead track and are guided by metal or nylon hardware screwed to the floor.

Cafe curtains. Short curtains that are often hung in tiers, usually from rods with rings. May also be gathered on a curtain rod for a semistationary treatment.

Cafe rings. Clip-on or sew-on rings from which cafe curtains are hung.

Canopy. An awning-shaped fabric window treatment installed on the upper portion of a window, usually with cafe curtains or shutters used below it.

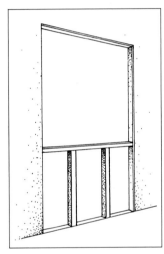

Casement window. A type of window that swings open and closed on side hinges, usually with the help of a crank-type operator.

Casing. Trim work whose purpose is to cover the joint between door jamb or window jamb material and the surrounding wall surface.

Clip-on pleats. Pleats pressed into a straight-hem heading and held in place with clip-on cafe curtain rings.

Combination rods. Two or three drapery rods on one pair of brackets, used for layered window treatments. Combination sets can include only traverse or both traverse and stationary rods.

Conventional traverse rod. A cord-controlled drapery rod. Both length and the distance it projects from the wall are adjustable. Available in two-way or one-way draw.

Cornice. A decorative wood unit installed at the top of a window treatment to hide drapery or curtain rods.

Cripples. Short studs above or below a window or door opening. They help shore up both the opening and the structure above or below, and also serve as a nailing surface for the wall material.

Custom-made treatments. More costly than ready-mades or made-to-measure treatments (see separate entries), custom treatments are made to fit one specific window. Usually ordered through a designer, custom treatments often call for custom track systems.

Dead bolt. A security device designed to increase the burglar-resistance of exterior doors. The end of a horizontal dead bolt fits snugly into the jamb; some drop vertically to stop all but the most persistent thief. A dead bolt must be operated with a key or knob; it doesn't lock automatically.

Decorative traverse rod. A cord-operated rod designed so draperies ride below it on decorative rings, allowing the rod to show whether the draperies are open or closed.

Double cylinder. A type of security lock that must be operated with a key from inside as well as outside.

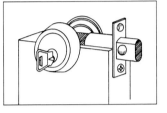

Double glazing. A two-pane-thick window or door glass (or plastic) designed to slow the passage of heat in and out. Can be two single panes with an air space between or a molded glazing with a vacuum-like air space. Sometimes called *insulating glass*.

Double-hung window. Two sashes move up and down. Older double-hungs are counter-balanced with rope-weight-and-pulley systems on either side of the window; newer windows utilize a pair of spring-lift devices instead.

Drapery hooks. Pin-on or slip-in hardware used to hang draperies from rods.

Draw draperies. Any drapery treatment designed to be used with a traverse rod, creating a window covering that can be drawn to open or close, either from both sides to the center or from one side to the other.

Fanlight. A semicircular window placed over a door or other window for decoration and additional light.

Finial. The ornament at the end of a decorative traverse rod, a cafe curtain rod, or a pole.

Fixed-glass windows. Non-operable sashes, either ready-made or custom-cut.

Flush door. A door with a flush surface, in contrast to the more textured panel door.

(continued)

GLOSSARY
(continued)

Glazing. A term often used in place of *glass* (although glazing is now loosely used to describe any clear window, whether acrylic, another synthetic, or glass). A window or door can be single-, double-, or triple-glazed, meaning that it has one, two, or three layers of glass in it. Glazing also refers to the act of installing glass in a sash.

Head. The top of a door or window opening.

Header. A doubled framing member laid on edge over a door, window, or other opening to provide support for the framing above the opening. It doubles as a nailing surface for window or door's top jamb.

Heading. The stiffened upper portion of a drapery panel or cafe-curtain panel.

Hinged door. One that swings on two and sometimes three hinges screwed to the jamb.

Holdbacks. Decorative window hardware, mounted on the wall to the side of the window or on the window frame.

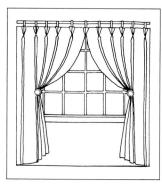

Used to secure the band, cord, or chain that ties back curtain or drapery panels, or by themselves, to hold panels directly.

Hopper window. An upside-down awning window hinged at the bottom instead of the top. Many basement windows are this type.

Inside mount. A window treatment that is installed between the jambs rather than on the casing.

Insulated glass. Double or triple glazing installed in many present-day windows and doors. It increases the R-value of the window 100 percent or more over standard window glass.

Jabots. The pieces of fabric that hang on either side of a swag or valance.

Jalousie. A type of window or storm door featuring a series of movable glass slats.

Jambs. The sides and top of a door or window opening. Swinging doors and casement windows are hinged from their side jambs.

Lambrequin. A decorative wood frame built around the top and sides of a window to create a larger, more impressive window treatment.

Latch. A mechanical device whose components come together to hold and sometimes lock a door or window.

Lockset. The hardware that keeps a door firmly closed. It usually comes packaged with all the needed components—a knob (sometimes fitted with a lock), latch, and strike plate.

Made-to-measure treatments. Generally midway between ready-made and custom-made treatments in cost. You provide a retailer with measurements and select from available fabric samples.

Master slides. The slides on a traverse rod that are in the center and have arms. They are the only ones attached to the cord, and they pull the drapery panels closed.

Mullion. A slender structural member between two windows. Trim that covers the gap between windows is called *mullion casing.*

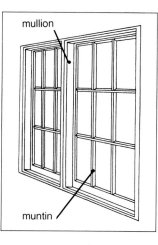

mullion

muntin

Muntins. Non-structural horizontal, vertical, or diagonal members that separate the panes in some windows. Also, in some newer windows, a wood or plastic grill that fits inside the window.

One-way draw. A conventional rod that closes left to right or right to left.

Outside mount. The installation of a window treatment on or beyond the window casing as opposed to an installation within the casing, referred to as an inside mount.

Overdraperies. The topmost drapery in a double or combination drapery treatment.

Overlap. The space at the center of two-way draw draperies where the two drapery panels overlap one another to assure privacy and a smooth installation.

Panel door. A door with panels framed by horizontal and vertical structural members. Most older doors are this type.

Parting strip (stop). One of a series of strips in the frame of a double-hung window that helps create the channel in

which the window sashes move up and down. It also provides the necessary clearance between the two sashes.

Pleating tape. A premarked tape used as stiffening for drapery headings.

Pocket door. A type of interior door that, when opened, slides back into a cavity created for it in the wall. It doesn't require any room clearance when opened.

Prehung door. A hinged door that comes partially assembled. Typically, the unit comes with jambs, stops, and hinges installed, the mortise for the strike plate cut in, and the lockset holes cut. Sometimes, even the casing is attached.

Priscilla curtains. A pair of ruffled tie-back curtains with attached valance.

Projection. The distance the front surface of a drapery or curtain rod is from the wall upon which it's mounted.

Rails. The horizontal members between the panels of a door. Typically, they are dadoed to accept the panels.

Ready-made treatments. Draperies and curtains manufactured in standard sizes and styles. This type of window treatment offers fewer choices than either custom-made or made-to-measure treatments, but convenience and lower cost are advantages.

Repeat. The distance between repetition of the complete design motif in a patterned fabric.

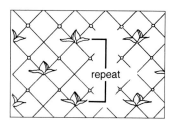

repeat

Replacement glass. Any glass used to repair a broken window.

Return. The portion of the drapery or curtain that covers the rod projection at each end.

Rod pocket curtains. Flat curtain panels with a pocket or casing sewn into them to receive the curtain rod.

Roller shade. Window treatments of fabric or other material attached to spring rollers installed either inside window casing or on window frame. Usually installed for privacy and light control and often used in combination with other window treatments.

Roman shade. A fabric window treatment that is raised and lowered in horizontal folds by means of a series of tapes to which rings, threaded with cord, are attached.

Rough opening. The framework into which a door or window will be installed.

Sash. That part of a window which opens and closes. It includes a frame and one or more panes of glass. Also, the frame and glass of a non-operable window.

Sash cord. A cord that attaches to a double-hung window sash on one end, passes over a pulley, and extends down the side of the window. A *sash weight* hangs from the end of the cord and acts as a counterbalance to the weight of the window, permitting easy movement of the sash. A *sash chain* is a metal version of a sash cord.

Sash curtains. Flat curtain panels gathered on rods that are attached to the sashes and move with them.

Sash rod. A flat curtain rod with almost no projection.

Sheers. Curtains or draperies made of translucent fabric, most often used under another, heavier treatment.

Shirred curtain. Technically, any curtain gathered onto a curtain rod, but the term is most often used for curtains that are gathered onto rods at both the top and bottom edges.

Sidelight. A glass panel adjacent to a door, often used at entries for appearance and to admit additional light.

Sill. The lowermost horizontal structural member of a window.

Skylight. A window of sorts in the roof that admits light from above. A skylight can be either operable or nonoperable; some are flat, others bubble-like.

Spring lift. A device fastened to the sashes and jambs of

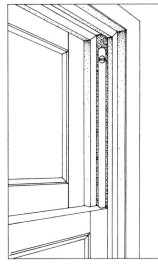

some newer double-hung windows. When wound sufficiently tight, it acts as a counterbalance to the window's weight.

Spring tension rod. Curtain rods designed to compress snugly inside a window frame.

Stack back. The area occupied by draperies when they are open.

Stationary rod. A non-operable rod from which a curtain or drapery panel is hung.

Stiles. The vertical uprights on either side (and occasionally between the panels) of a panel door.

Stool. The piece of trim at the base of a window onto which the lower sash comes to rest.

Stop. Door or window molding that prevents movement beyond the desired point.

Strike. A metal plate fastened to the jamb on the latch side of a door. It accepts the latch or dead bolt when the door is closed.

Support. A drapery hardware unit designed to support the weight of long traverse rods.

Swag. Festoon or draped fabric used above a traditional window treatment. Usually used in combination with jabots.

Tieback. A fabric band, cord, or chain used to hold drapery or curtain panels away from the center of the window.

Tiered curtains. Usually cafe curtains, hung in two or more tiers with the top curtains slightly overlapping the lower curtains.

Transom. A window above a door or other window, sometimes hinged so that it is oper-

able. Also, the horizontal crossbar in a window or over a door that separates the lower opening from the transom or fanlight above.

Traverse rod. A drapery rod that allows you to open and close a fabric treatment.

Trimmers. Studs on either side of a door, window, or other opening that support the header. They also serve as the *jamb studs* to which door and window jambs are attached.

Two-way draw. A conventional traverse rod that allows the draperies hung from it to pull closed from both sides to the center.

Underdraperies. Draperies used under a decorative treatment (which may be stationary or operable), usually for privacy and light control. Often made of translucent fabric.

Valance. Decorative panel of fabric hung at the top of draperies or curtains to hide the window hardware.

Venetian blind. Window treatment made up of horizontal slats that may be tilted for light control and privacy. Blinds are raised or lowered by means of a pull cord. Mini-slat blinds have narrower slats.

Vertical blind. The same principle as a venetian blind, but with slats running up and down instead of left to right. Installed on a track mounted on the ceiling, floor, or above the window.

Woven woods. A window treatment that combines wood slats and yarn in the form of roller shades, Roman shades, cafe curtains, draperies, or panels to be hung from a custom-made heading system.

WHERE TO GO FOR MORE INFORMATION

Better Homes and Gardens® Books

Would you like to learn more about decorating, remodeling, or maintaining your windows and doors? These Better Homes and Gardens® books can help.

Better Homes and Gardens®
NEW DECORATING BOOK
How to translate ideas into workable solutions for every room in your home. Choosing a style, furniture arrangements, windows, walls and ceilings, floors, lighting, and accessories. 433 color photos, 76 how-to illustrations, 432 pages.

Better Homes and Gardens®
COMPLETE GUIDE TO HOME REPAIR,
MAINTENANCE, & IMPROVEMENT
Inside your home, outside your home, your home's systems, basics you should know. Anatomy and step-by-step drawings illustrate components, tools, techniques, and finishes.
515 how-to techniques; 75 charts; 2,734 illustrations; 552 pages.

Better Homes and Gardens®
COMPLETE GUIDE TO GARDENING
A comprehensive guide for beginners and experienced gardeners. Houseplants, lawns and landscaping, trees and shrubs, greenhouses, insects and diseases. 461 color photos, 434 how-to illustrations, 37 charts, 552 pages.

Better Homes and Gardens®
STEP-BY-STEP BUILDING SERIES
A series of do-it-yourself building books that provides step-by-step illustrations and how-to information for starting and finishing many common construction projects and repair jobs around your house. More than 90 projects and 1,200 illustrations in this series of six 96-page books:
STEP-BY-STEP BASIC PLUMBING
STEP-BY-STEP BASIC WIRING
STEP-BY-STEP BASIC CARPENTRY
STEP-BY-STEP HOUSEHOLD REPAIRS
STEP-BY-STEP MASONRY & CONCRETE
STEP-BY-STEP CABINETS AND SHELVES

Other Sources of Information

Many manufacturers publish catalogs, style books, or product brochures that are available upon request.

Andersen Windowalls
Bayport, MN 55003

Bali Blinds
425 E. 61st St.
New York, NY 10021

Blaine Window Hardware, Inc.
1919 Blaine Dr., RD 4
Hagerstown, MD 21740

Caradco Corporation
(windows)
A Subsidiary of Bendix
P.O. Box 920
Rantoul, IL 61866

Clopay
Window Covering Division
Clopay Square
Cincinnati, OH 45214

Flexalum Blinds
(window treatments)
Window Products Div.
20 Campus Rd.
Totowa, NJ 07511

Graber (drapery hardware)
Graber Plaza
Middleton, WI 53562

Insulated Steel Door Systems
1230 Keith Building
Cleveland, OH 44115

Interior Window Coverings, Inc.
209 East Baltimore
Detroit, MI 48202

Joanna Western Mills Co.
(window treatments)
2141 S. Jefferson St.
Chicago, IL 60616

Joseph C. Klein, Inc.
(windows)
Rotterdam Industrial Park
Schenectady, NY 12306

Kenney Manufacturing Co.
(drapery hardware)
Warwick, RI 02887

Kirsch (drapery hardware)
309 Prospect
Sturgis, MI 49091

Levolor Lorentzen, Inc.
(window treatments)
720 Monroe St.
Hoboken, NJ 07030

Louverdrape, Inc.
(window treatments)
1100 Colorado Ave.
Santa Monica, CA 90401

Newell Companies, Inc.
(drapery hardware)
Freeport, IL 61032

Pella Rolscreen Manufacturing
Company
(windows and doors)
100 Main St.
Pella, IA 50219

Perma-Door by Steelcraft
An American Standard Co.
9017 Blue Ash Road
Cincinnati, OH 45242

PPG Industries (energy-saving
window treatments)
1 Gateway Center
Pittsburgh, PA 15222

The Renovator's Supply, Inc.
Renovator's Old Mill
Millers Falls, MA 01349

Fred Reuton, Inc. (windows)
Closter, NJ 07624

Simpson Timber Company
(doors)
Fabricated Products Division
2506 Multnomah St.
Portland, OR 97212

Stanley Door Systems
Division of the Stanley Works
2400 East Lincoln Rd.
Birmingham, MI 48012

Stanley Drapery Hardware
Division of the Stanley Works
Wallingford, CT 06492

St. Regis Forest Products
(doors)
1019 Pacific Ave.
Tacoma, WA 98401

U.S. Plywood (doors)
A Division of Champion
International
777 Third Ave.
New York, NY 10017

ACKNOWLEDGMENTS

Architects and Designers

The following is a listing by page of the interior designers, architects, and project designers whose work appears in this book.

Cover:
Turnkey Living/Valya

Pages 6-7
Allan W. Wall, A.I.A.

Pages 8-9
Corrinne Appleby

Pages 10-11
Karen Marcus, Halls Crown Center

Pages 12-13
Ilene Sanford

Pages 14-15
Turnkey Living/Valya

Pages 16-17
Gary Bressler;
Martin R. Lunde

Pages 18-19
Stewart S. Farnett, A.I.A.

Pages 20-31
David Howard

Pages 34-35
Gordon Little, A.S.I.D.

Pages 36-37
Robert E. Dittmer;
Eve Victor Interiors

Pages 38-39
Suzanne Branham;
Karin Weller

Pages 40-41
Gardiner Rapelye, Jr.

Pages 42-43
William Seales, Gallery Five Interiors;
Norman's of Salisbury

Pages 44-45
Roz Main, F.A.S.I.D.;
Francoise Moros

Pages 46-47
Camille Lehman;
Suzy Taylor

Pages 48-49
Jack Metherell;
Diane Vogel, A.S.I.D. and Jane Kohl

Pages 52-53
Sharon Richtor

Pages 54-55
Joann L. Hanson;
Marlene Grant, A.S.I.D.

Pages 58-59
Sims Murray;
David W. Durrant

Pages 60-61
Ernest Barth

Pages 62-63
Florence Forster, Design Associates;
Deborah Dooley

Pages 64-73
Jill Mead

Pages 90-91
Charles Stinson;
Christine Garrett;
Scruggs/Myers & Associates

Pages 104-105
Judy Tretheway

Pages 112-113
Jane Griswold

Pages 124-125
Miriam O'Day;
Cynthia Thurber;
Jane and Paul Juliet

Pages 126-127
Don Beletsky, Otis Associates;
Jane Phibbs

Pages 128-129
Cathy Simon, Marquis Assoc., A.I.A.;
Peter Falck, A.I.A.

Pages 134-135
Kirby Ward Fitzpatrick, A.I.A., Karen/Seals Architects, Inc.

Pages 136-137
Dale Hollingsworth, A.S.I.D., Baker, Knapp & Tubb Showroom

Pages 138-139
Cathy Simon, Marquis Associates, A.I.A.;
John Milnes Baker

Photographers and Illustrators

We extend our thanks to the following photographers and illustrators, whose creative talents and technical skills contributed to this book.

Ernest Braun
Jim Buckels
Ross Chapple
Mike Dieter
Mike Eagleton
Feliciano
Gorcher & Gorcher
Harry Hartman
Bob Hawks
Bill Hedrich, Hedrich-Blessing
Thomas E. Hooper
Bill Hopkins, Jr.
William N. Hopkins
Tom Rosborough
Fred Lyon
Bill Maris, Maris/Semel
Frank Lotz Miller
Carson Ode
Steve Shock, Hellman Design Associates
Ozzie Sweet
Jessie Walker

Manufacturers

We appreciate the assistance of the following companies in preparing this book.

Country Curtains
Kirsch Company
Levolor Lorentzen, Inc.
NRG International
The Renovator's Supply, Inc.
Reynolds Metals Co.
Schlage
Sears, Roebuck and Company
Serrande of Italy
3M Energy Control Products

YOUR WINDOWS AND DOORS

INDEX

Page numbers in *italics* refer to illustrations or illustrated text.

INDEX
(continued)